101 More Things To Do With Bacon

101 Things More To Do With Bacon

BY ELIZA CROSS

GIBBS SMITH
TO ENRICH AND INSPIRE HUMANKIND

First Edition
20 19 18 17 16   5 4 3 2 1

101 Things is a registered trademark of Gibbs Smith, Publisher
and Stephanie Ashcraft.

Published by
Gibbs Smith
P.O. Box 667
Layton, Utah 84041

1.800.835.4993 orders
www.gibbs-smith.com
Printed and bound in Korea

Gibbs Smith books are printed on either recycled, 100% post-consumer
waste, FSC-certified papers or on paper produced from sustainable PEFC-
certified forest/controlled wood source. Learn more at www.pefc.org.

Library of Congress Cataloging-in-Publication Data
Library of Congress Control Number: 2016933631
ISBN 13: 978-1-4236-4392-0

For Jose Luis Castaneda

CONTENTS

Salads

Chinese Crunch Salad 66 • Warm Bacon and Chicken Ranch Salad 67 • Creamy Avocado, Bacon, and Sweet Corn Salad 68 • Broccoli and Bacon Salad 69 • German Bacon Slaw 70 • Best Bacon Macaroni Salad 71 • Spring Greens with Apples, Bacon, and Gorgonzola 72 • Perfect Wedge Salad 73 • Warm Bacon Potato Salad with Sour Cream Dressing 74 • Watercress Salad with Bacon, Crab, and Avocado 75

Sandwiches

BLEST Sandwiches (Bacon, Lettuce, Egg Salad, and Tomato) 78 • Bacon-Wrapped Cheese Dogs 79 • Cobb Clubs 80 • Bacon Crab Melts 81 • Bacon and Turkey Grilled Cheese 82 • Bacon Buffalo Chicken Wraps 83 • Grilled B.A.M. Sandwiches (Bacon, Avocado, and Muenster) 84 • The Elvis Special 85 • Slow Cooker Bacon Barbecue Chicken Rolls 86 • Bacon Mushroom Melts 87

Side Dishes

Bacon-Wrapped Corn on the Cob 90 • Bacon and Parmesan Hasselback Potatoes 91 • Crunchy Bacon and Onion Snow Peas 92 • Bacon and Mushroom Stuffing 93 • Brussels Sprouts with Bacon 94 • Bacon Pull-Apart Bread 95 • Bacon and Asparagus Saute 96 • Bacon Roasted Butternut Squash 97 • Bacon-Stuffed Artichokes 98 • Green Beans with Bacon, Maple, and Pecans 99 • Sweet Potato, Bacon, and Apple Casserole 100

Dinners

Glazed Bacon Dijon Pork Tenderloin 102 • Bacon Chicken Jalapeno Popper Casserole 103 • Bacon BBQ Brisket 104 • Ultimate Bacon-Wrapped Turkey 105 • Bacon, Spinach, and Tomato Cheese Tortellini 106 • Pesto Bacon Chicken 107 • Bacon Beef Burgundy 108 • Creamy Bacon Corn Shrimp Risotto 109 • Bacon Cheeseburger Soft Tacos 110 • Bacon Pepper Jack Mac and Cheese 111 • Bacon-Wrapped Chicken Pinwheels 112 • Bacon, Beef, and Bean Casserole 113 • Bacon, Chicken, and Noodles 114 • Bacon Garlic Butter Scallops 115 • Smothered Bacon and Onion Chicken 116 • BLT Bow Tie Pasta 117 • Slow Cooker Heavenly Bacon Chicken 118

Desserts and Sweets

Bacon Peanut Butter Cookies 120 • Man Candy 121 • Bacon Walnut Maple Fudge 122 • Bacon Bread Pudding with Vanilla Sauce 123 • Maple Bacon Crunch 124 • Bacon Mincemeat Tarts 125

HELPFUL HINTS

I. In general, regular sliced bacon is about $1/16$ inch thick, and a pound contains 16–20 strips. A pound of thick-sliced bacon is about $1/8$ inch thick and contains 12–16 strips per pound. The recipes in this cookbook call for regular sliced bacon unless otherwise indicated.

2. Nitrate-free bacon is sometimes saltier than regular bacon due to processing. Adjust salt accordingly if using nitrate-free bacon for the recipes in this book.

3. Artisanal bacon is made from fresh pork bellies that are slowly cured and smoked over a wood fire. Due to its handmade nature, the strips may be more irregular in shape.

4. Dry-cured bacon has a more intense pork flavor; it also contains less water and tends to shrink less during cooking.

5. Flavored bacons contain additives like apple cider, maple syrup, brown sugar, and pepper. Sweet flavorings may decrease bacon's cooking time and increase the risk of burning, so cook at a lower temperature and watch carefully.

6. Bacon smoked over hardwood develops a distinct flavor. Woods like apple, maple, and cherry give the bacon a slightly sweet flavor, while hickory and oak impart a strong, hearty taste.

7. To store bacon, first wrap it airtight in waxed paper or plastic wrap and then cover it tightly with aluminum foil. Keep it in the coolest part of the refrigerator.

8. For the best flavor, plan to use bacon within 7 days of opening the package.

9. Bacon can be frozen for up to 1 month. Thaw in the refrigerator overnight before using.

10. To fry bacon, arrange the strips in a heavy unheated frying pan and fry over moderate heat. Use a bacon press to cook it evenly and keep it from curling.

11. For easy, mess-proof cooking, bake bacon in a 350 degree oven. Arrange the strips on a broiler pan and cook 15–20 minutes to desired crispness.

12. To microwave, arrange bacon strips on 4 layers of paper towels, cover with 2 more paper towels, and cook at 70% power for about 1 minute per strip, watching carefully to avoid overcooking.

13. Bacon cooked at a lower temperature tends to curl less than when cooked at high temperatures.

14. For recipes that call for securing bacon with toothpicks during baking or grilling, soak the toothpicks in water for at least 1 hour to avoid charring.

15. To reuse leftover bacon grease, cool it to room temperature and pour it through a strainer into a heatproof container. Cover and store in the refrigerator.

16. Never pour bacon grease down the drain as it can solidify and cause clogs. Instead, pour it into an old can or other container before disposing.

17. Unless otherwise specified, these recipes were tested with large eggs, unsalted butter, and all-purpose flour.

BREAKFASTS

BACON PECAN STICKY BUNS

6 strips	**bacon,** cut in $1/4$-inch pieces
$1/2$ cup	**butter,** softened, divided
$2/3$ cup	**packed dark brown sugar,** divided
$1/2$ cup	**chopped pecans**
I sheet	**packaged frozen puff pastry,** thawed
I $1/2$ teaspoons	**cinnamon**

Preheat oven to 400 degrees. Line a baking sheet with parchment paper. Cook the bacon in a large frying pan over medium heat until most of the fat has rendered. Transfer bacon to paper towels and drain; reserve.

In a medium bowl, cream together 7 tablespoons butter with $1/3$ cup brown sugar until light and fluffy, about 2 minutes. Divide the mixture between the cups of a 12-cup nonstick muffin pan. Divide the chopped pecans and cooked bacon between the cups.

Melt the remaining I tablespoon butter. Unfold the sheet of puff pastry onto a lightly floured work surface with the folds opening left to right. Brush with the melted butter and sprinkle evenly with remaining $1/3$ cup brown sugar and the cinnamon. Starting at the bottom edge, tightly roll up the pastry and pinch the seam to seal. Cut the roll into 12 equal pieces. Arrange pieces with spiral facing up in the muffin cups.

Bake for 15–20 minutes, or until golden brown and firm to the touch. Remove from the oven and cool in the pan for 5 minutes; immediately invert pan on prepared baking sheet, scraping any remaining sauce from the cups and spreading it on top of the buns. Let the buns cool slightly before serving. Makes 12 buns.

BACON AND EGG TURNOVERS

8	**eggs,** divided
I tablespoon	**butter**
$^1/_4$ cup	**finely chopped onion**
4 ounces	**cream cheese,** softened
I pound	**bacon,** cooked and crumbled
$^1/_4$ teaspoon	**salt**
$^1/_4$ teaspoon	**pepper**
I sheet	**packaged frozen puff pastry,** thawed
I tablespoon	**water**

Preheat oven to 400 degrees. Prepare a large baking sheet with nonstick cooking spray.

In a large bowl, beat 7 of the eggs; reserve. In a large frying pan, melt the butter over medium heat. Add the onion and cook, stirring, until translucent, about 5 minutes. Add the beaten eggs and cook, stirring occasionally, until soft curds form. Add the cream cheese and cook for I minute, stirring until combined. Add the bacon, salt, and pepper, and stir to incorporate. Transfer the mixture to a bowl and cool to room temperature.

On a lightly floured surface, roll out the puff pastry to a 16-inch square and cut in 4 equal squares. Divide the egg mixture evenly on each square, just slightly off center. In a small bowl, beat the remaining egg with the water. Brush the edges of each pastry square with the beaten egg and fold over to form 4 triangles. Crimp the edges with the tines of a fork to seal. Transfer the turnovers to prepared baking sheet and brush the tops with the remaining beaten egg. Bake until golden, about 25 minutes. Let cool slightly before serving. Makes 4 servings.

APPLE BACON STRATA

3 tablespoons	**butter**
2 medium	**Granny Smith apples,** peeled, cored, and chopped
$1/4$ cup	**packed dark brown sugar**
$1/2$ teaspoon	**cinnamon**
6 cups	**cubed day-old French bread**
1 pound	**bacon,** cooked and crumbled
5	**eggs**
$2 1/4$ cups	**milk**
$1/4$ teaspoon	**salt**
1 cup	**maple syrup**
$1/2$ cup	**chopped, toasted pecans**

In a large frying pan, melt butter over medium heat. Add the apples and cook, stirring occasionally, until crisp-tender, about 3 minutes. Reduce heat to medium-low and sprinkle with brown sugar and cinnamon. Cook, stirring occasionally, until apples are tender, about 8 minutes. Remove from heat and cool to room temperature.

Prepare an 8 x 8-inch baking dish with nonstick cooking spray and arrange half of the bread cubes evenly in the bottom. Top with half of the bacon, and then half of the apples. Repeat layers. In a large bowl, whisk together the eggs, milk, and salt, and pour evenly over the strata. Cover and refrigerate for at least 2 hours, or overnight.

Preheat oven to 350 degrees and bake for 45–55 minutes, or until puffed, golden, and a knife inserted near the center comes out clean. Let stand 15 minutes before serving.

In a small saucepan, heat the syrup and pecans until warmed, stirring once. Drizzle sauce over the strata when ready to serve. Makes 9 servings.

BACON AND EGG POTATO SKINS

4	**large russet potatoes,** baked
2 tablespoons	**butter,** melted
8	**eggs**
	salt and pepper, to taste
8 strips	**bacon,** cooked and crumbled
3/4 cup	**grated sharp cheddar cheese,** divided
2 tablespoons	**chopped flat-leaf parsley**

Preheat oven to 350 degrees. Line a large baking sheet with aluminum foil. Slice the potatoes in half lengthwise, and scoop out the interior of each half to make a shell, leaving about 1/2 inch of potato attached to the skin. Arrange the shells on prepared baking sheet. (Use the scooped-out potato for another purpose such as mashed potatoes.)

Drizzle 1/8 of the melted butter into each potato shell. Divide and sprinkle 1/2 cup of cheese evenly among the 8 shells. Gently break an egg into a small dish and slide it into a potato; repeat with remaining eggs and potatoes. Season each egg with salt and pepper, and top with the crumbled bacon. Bake until the eggs are set, about 20–25 minutes. During the last 5 minutes of baking, remove from oven and sprinkle remaining cheese evenly over the top of the potatoes. Finish baking until cheese melts and remove from oven. Cool for 5 minutes and garnish with parsley before serving. Makes 8 servings.

BROWN SUGAR AND BACON PANCAKES

1 cup	**flour**
1 tablespoon	**sugar**
1 teaspoon	**baking powder**
1/4 teaspoon	**baking soda**
1/4 teaspoon	**salt**
1 cup	**buttermilk**
1	**egg**
1 teaspoon	**vanilla**
2 tablespoons	**butter,** melted
	vegetable oil
1/2 pound	**bacon,** cooked and crumbled
	light brown sugar, for sprinkling

Whisk flour, sugar, baking powder, baking soda, and salt in a medium bowl to combine.

In a separate bowl, whisk together the buttermilk, egg, vanilla, and butter until combined. Make a well in the center of the flour mixture and slowly pour in the buttermilk mixture, whisking gently just until combined (a few lumps will remain). Do not overmix.

Brush a griddle lightly with oil and heat over medium heat. Working in batches, pour the batter on the griddle, using 1/4 cup for each pancake. Sprinkle each pancake evenly with 1 heaping teaspoon of crumbled bacon. Cook pancakes for about 1 minute on each side until golden brown, turning when top surface bubbles and is dotted with holes. Transfer the pancakes to a heated platter and sprinkle with light brown sugar. Makes about 12 pancakes.

JALAPENO BACON POPPER QUICHE

1 (9-inch)	**pie crust**
$^1/_2$ cup	**cream cheese,** softened
3	**medium jalapenos,** divided
$^1/_2$ cup	**heavy cream**
$^1/_2$ cup	**half-and-half**
5	**eggs**
1 teaspoon	**paprika**
$^1/_4$ teaspoon	**salt**
4 strips	**bacon,** cooked and crumbled
$^1/_2$ cup	**grated cheddar cheese**

Preheat oven to 400 degrees. Fit the pie crust into a 9-inch pie pan. Prick the crust all over the bottom and sides with a fork and bake for 10 minutes. Remove from oven to a wire rack and lower oven temperature to 350 degrees. Spread the cream cheese evenly on the bottom of the warm pie crust. Seed and dice 2 of the jalapenos and sprinkle over the cream cheese.

In a small saucepan, combine the cream and half-and-half, and cook over medium heat until small bubbles appear around the edge of the pan, about 5 minutes.

Whisk the eggs together in a large bowl. Slowly add the hot cream mixture to the eggs, whisking constantly to combine. Add the paprika, salt, and bacon, and pour into the crust. Bake for 30 minutes. Seed and cut the remaining jalapeno in $^1/_8$-inch slices. Remove quiche from oven and arrange jalapeno slices on top. Sprinkle with cheese and continue baking until quiche is golden brown, about 15 minutes. Cool slightly before slicing and serving. Makes 6 servings.

BACON AND EGG SUNRISE CUPS

12 strips	**bacon**
6 slices	**bread**
12	**eggs**
1/2 cup	**grated cheddar cheese**

Preheat oven to 400 degrees. Prepare a 12-cup muffin pan with nonstick cooking spray.

Heat a frying pan on medium-high heat and cook the bacon until lightly browned but still flexible. Transfer bacon to paper towels to drain; reserve. Using a 2-inch biscuit cutter, cut 2 circles from each bread slice and fit in the bottom of each of the muffin cups. Wrap a bacon strip around the inside of each muffin cup. Evenly divide and sprinkle cheese over the bread.

Crack each egg gently, one at a time, into a small bowl and slide it in a muffin cup. Bake until whites have set and yolk is cooked, about 10–15 minutes. Makes 6 servings.

MINI BACON BREAKFAST TARTS

8 ounces	**cream cheese,** softened
2	**eggs**
2 tablespoons	**milk**
1/4 cup	**grated sharp cheddar cheese**
1/4 cup	**grated Parmesan cheese**
2 tablespoons	**chopped green onion**
1 can (10 ounces)	**refrigerated flaky biscuits**
6 strips	**bacon,** cooked and crumbled, divided

Preheat oven to 375 degrees. Prepare 10 muffin cups with nonstick cooking spray.

Combine the cream cheese, eggs, and milk in a medium bowl and beat together until combined, about 1 minute. Stir in the cheddar cheese, Parmesan cheese, and green onion; reserve.

Separate dough into 10 biscuits. Press 1 biscuit into the bottom and 1/2 inch up the sides of each muffin cup. Sprinkle half of the bacon evenly among the cups. Spoon about 2 tablespoons of the cream cheese mixture into each cup.

Bake 20–25 minutes, or until filling is set and tarts are browned. Remove from the oven and sprinkle with the remaining bacon, lightly pressing into filling. Cool for 5 minutes before serving. Makes 10 tarts.

BACON, SWISS CHEESE, AND CHIVE OMELETS

8	**eggs**
1/2 teaspoon	**salt,** divided
1/2 teaspoon	**pepper,** divided
2 tablespoons	**butter,** melted
2/3 cup	**grated Swiss cheese**
8 strips	**bacon,** cooked and crumbled
3 tablespoons	**finely chopped chives**

Preheat an omelet pan or small frying pan over medium heat.

In a small bowl, whisk together 2 of the eggs with 1/8 teaspoon salt and 1/8 teaspoon pepper. Lightly brush the inside of the pan with 1/4 of the melted butter, and pour in the eggs. Cook, tilting and swirling the pan occasionally while lightly scraping the pan sides with a spatula until the eggs are just set, 1–2 minutes. Sprinkle 1/4 of the cheese, bacon, and chives over 1/2 of the eggs. Use the spatula to gently fold the eggs in half to form an omelet. Repeat with remaining eggs, cheese, bacon, and chives. Wipe out the pan with a paper towel between preparing each omelet. Makes 4 servings.

APPLE AND BACON BREAKFAST BARS

I cup	**rolled oats**
$^1/_2$ cup	**flour**
$^1/_2$ cup	**packed dark brown sugar**
$^1/_2$ teaspoon	**cinnamon**
$^1/_4$ teaspoon	**baking powder**
$^1/_4$ teaspoon	**salt**
$^1/_8$ teaspoon	**nutmeg**
6 tablespoons	**unsalted butter,** melted
I cup	**prepared apple pie filling**
5 strips	**bacon,** cooked and crumbled

Preheat oven to 350 degrees. Prepare a 9 x 9-inch baking dish with nonstick cooking spray.

In a medium bowl, stir together the oats, flour, brown sugar, cinnamon, baking powder, salt, and nutmeg until well combined. Drizzle in the melted butter and stir with a fork until evenly moistened. Measure out $^1/_2$ cup of the mixture and reserve. Spread the rest of the mixture in the prepared baking dish and use fingers to press it evenly into the bottom. Bake for 15 minutes.

While bars are baking, pour the apple pie filling in a food processor or blender and process until smooth. Remove bars from oven and spread the filling evenly over top. Sprinkle the bacon over the filling and then top with the reserved oat mixture. Return to the oven and continue baking until lightly browned, about 12–15 minutes. Remove from oven and cool in the pan on a wire rack for 30 minutes before cutting into 2 x 4-inch bars. Serve at once, or store in refrigerator, tightly wrapped, for up to 3 days. Makes 8 bars.

POTATO NESTS WITH EGGS AND BACON

15 ounces (about 4 cups) **frozen shredded hash browns,** thawed
1 1/2 cups **grated cheddar cheese,** divided
1 tablespoon **olive oil**
1/4 teaspoon **salt,** plus extra for sprinkling
1/4 teaspoon **pepper,** plus extra for sprinkling
8 **eggs**
4 strips **bacon,** cooked and crumbled
2 teaspoons **chopped flat-leaf parsley**

Preheat oven to 425 degrees. Lightly spray 8 cups of a muffin pan with nonstick cooking spray.

In a large bowl, combine the hash browns, 1 cup cheese, olive oil, salt, and pepper, and stir until mixed together. Divide the mixture evenly among the 8 muffin cups, and use your fingers to press the mixture into the bottom and up the sides of the cups. Bake until edges are browned and the cheese has melted, about 15 minutes. Cool in the pan 5 minutes and reduce oven temperature to 350 degrees.

Crack each egg gently into a small bowl and slide into a potato nest. Sprinkle each with salt and pepper, to taste. Divide bacon among the 8 nests, and top with remaining 1/2 cup cheese. Return to oven and bake until egg whites are set, and yolks are cooked to your liking, about 12–16 minutes. Remove from oven and cool in the pan for 5 minutes. Slide a knife around the edges and use a fork to gently lift nests from pan. Garnish with chopped parsley. Makes 8 servings.

CHILE RELLENO AND BACON BAKE

2 cans (4 ounces each)	**diced green chiles,** drained
I cup	**grated sharp cheddar cheese**
$^1/_2$ cup	**grated Monterey Jack cheese**
8 strips	**bacon,** cooked and crumbled
5	**eggs**
3 cups	**milk**
I cup	**flour**
$^1/_2$ teaspoon	**salt**
$^1/_2$ teaspoon	**pepper**
$^1/_2$ teaspoon	**paprika**

Preheat oven to 350 degrees. Prepare a 9 x 13-inch baking dish with nonstick cooking spray.

In a medium bowl, mix together the chiles, cheddar cheese, Monterey Jack cheese, and bacon. Spread evenly in the bottom of prepared dish.

In a medium bowl, whisk together the eggs, milk, flour, salt, and pepper. Pour over chiles and cheese. Sprinkle paprika evenly over top. Bake until eggs are cooked through and a toothpick inserted into the center comes out clean, about 40–45 minutes. Cool for 5 minutes before serving. Makes 6 servings.

BACON STRIP GRIDDLE CAKES

1 1/4 cups	**flour**
1 tablespoon	**baking powder**
1 tablespoon	**sugar**
1/2 teaspoon	**salt**
1 cup	**milk**
2 tablespoons	**vegetable oil**
1	**egg**
8 strips	**bacon**
	softened butter
	maple syrup

In a large bowl, whisk together the flour, baking powder, sugar, and salt. In a medium bowl, whisk together the milk, oil, and egg until combined. Add the milk mixture to the flour mixture and stir just until combined. Batter will be slightly lumpy.

Heat a griddle over medium heat and cook the bacon strips until crispy. Transfer bacon to paper towels to drain, and discard all but 2 teaspoons of pan drippings; return pan to heat.

Working in batches, arrange 2 bacon strips on griddle and slowly pour about 1/4 cup batter over each strip to cover. Cook pancakes for about 1 minute on each side, or until golden brown, turning when top surface bubbles and is dotted with holes. Transfer the pancakes to a heated platter and repeat. Serve warm with butter and maple syrup. Makes about 8 pancakes.

BACON ARTICHOKE BRUNCH RING

I can (8 ounces)	**refrigerated crescent dinner rolls**
8 strips	**bacon**
1/3 cup plus I tablespoon	**milk,** divided
4	**eggs**
1/4 teaspoon	**salt**
1/4 teaspoon	**pepper**
1/2 cup	**chopped cooked artichoke hearts**
1/4 cup	**chopped red bell pepper**
I cup	**grated Monterey Jack cheese,** divided

Preheat oven to 375 degrees. Line a large baking sheet with parchment paper. Unroll dough and separate into 8 triangles. Arrange triangles in a starburst shape on baking sheet with short sides toward center, overlapping and leaving a 4-inch round opening in the center.

In a large frying pan, cook bacon over medium heat until lightly browned but not crisp, about 4–5 minutes, turning once. Transfer bacon to paper towels to drain, and discard all but 2 teaspoons of pan drippings. Return pan to heat.

In a medium bowl, whisk together 1/3 cup milk, eggs, salt, and pepper until combined. Stir in artichoke hearts and bell pepper. Pour egg mixture into frying pan; cook and stir until eggs are set, 4–5 minutes.

Place the bacon strips down the length of each triangle and sprinkle the widest part of the dough (towards the center) evenly with 1/3 cup cheese. Spoon the eggs over the cheese and sprinkle with 1/3 cup cheese. Pull points of triangles over eggs and cheese, and tuck under dough to form ring (filling will be visible). Brush dough with I tablespoon milk and top with 1/3 cup cheese. Bake until golden brown, about 20–25 minutes. Cool on pan for 2 minutes before serving. Makes 8 servings.

BACON FRENCH TOAST MUFFINS WITH MAPLE BUTTER

3	**eggs**
1 1/4 cups	**milk**
1 teaspoon	**sugar**
1/2 teaspoon	**cinnamon**
1/8 teaspoon	**salt**
5 cups	**cubed day-old bread**
6 strips	**bacon,** cooked and finely crumbled
6 tablespoons	**butter,** softened
2 tablespoons	**maple syrup**

In a large bowl, whisk together the eggs, milk, sugar, cinnamon, and salt until well combined. Add bread cubes and mix well to coat. Set aside for 20 minutes, stirring occasionally.

Preheat oven to 350 degrees. Prepare 6 cups of a jumbo muffin pan with nonstick cooking spray. Divide 1/3 of the bread-egg mixture between the cups. Sprinkle with half the bacon, pressing mixture into cups. Divide the remaining bread mixture among the cups and sprinkle with the remaining bacon, using fingers to lightly mound. Bake until mixture is set and muffins are golden brown, about 15–20 minutes.

In a small dish, stir together the butter and maple syrup; reserve at room temperature. Remove muffins from oven, and cool on a wire rack for 5 minutes before removing from pan. Serve with maple butter. Makes 6 servings.

BACON TATER TOT BREAKFAST BAKE

1 pound	**ground breakfast sausage,** cooked and crumbled
1 pound	**bacon,** cooked and crumbled
2 1/2 cups	**grated sharp cheddar cheese,** divided
2 cups	**whole milk**
3	**eggs**
1/2 teaspoon	**onion powder**
1/2 teaspoon	**pepper**
1/8 teaspoon	**salt**
1 pinch	**cayenne pepper**
2 pounds	**frozen tater tots**
2 tablespoons	**chopped flat-leaf parsley**

Preheat oven to 350 degrees.

Sprinkle the sausage evenly in the bottom of a 9 x 13-inch baking dish. Top with 1/2 of the bacon, and 2 cups of cheese.

In a large bowl, whisk together the milk, eggs, onion powder, pepper, salt, and cayenne pepper. Pour mixture evenly over the cheese in baking dish and arrange tater tots over top. Cook for 35 minutes and remove from oven. Top with remaining bacon and 1/2 cup cheese and continue baking until bubbling and golden brown, about 5–10 more minutes. Cool on a wire rack for 10 minutes before serving and garnish with chopped parsley. Makes 8–10 servings.

BACON CORNCAKES

I cup	**yellow cornmeal**
¹/₂ cup	**flour**
I tablespoon	**sugar**
2 teaspoons	**baking powder**
¹/₄ teaspoon	**salt**
I pinch	**cayenne pepper**
I cup	**fresh or frozen corn kernels,** thawed if using frozen
2	**eggs**
³/₄ cup	**milk**
2 tablespoons	**butter,** melted
6 strips	**bacon,** cooked and crumbled
	vegetable oil
	maple syrup

In a large bowl whisk together the cornmeal, flour, sugar, baking powder, salt, and cayenne pepper.

In a food processor, pulse the corn to make a coarse puree and transfer to a medium bowl. Whisk in the eggs, milk, and butter. Add the corn mixture to the cornmeal mixture, and stir just until combined. Let the batter stand, covered, for 10 minutes. Stir in the crumbled bacon.

Brush a griddle lightly with vegetable oil and heat over medium heat. Working in batches, pour the batter on the griddle, using ¹/₄ cup for each corncake. Cook for about 1 minute on each side, or until the top surface bubbles and is dotted with holes. Serve hot with maple syrup. Makes 4 servings.

BACON AND ASPARAGUS BREAKFAST CASSEROLE

8 cups	**water**
I pound	**fresh asparagus,** trimmed and cut in 1-inch pieces
4	**English muffins,** split and toasted
2 cups	**grated cheddar cheese,** divided
I pound	**bacon,** cooked and crumbled
1/2 cup	**chopped red bell pepper**
8	**eggs**
2 cups	**milk**
I teaspoon	**dry mustard**
I teaspoon	**salt**
1/4 teaspoon	**pepper**

Fill a large metal bowl with ice and water and reserve. In a large saucepan, bring 8 cups water to a boil over medium-high heat. Add the asparagus and cook just until crisp-tender, 2–3 minutes. Drain and place in ice water for I minute. Drain and transfer asparagus to paper towels; pat dry.

Prepare a 9 x 13-inch baking dish with nonstick cooking spray and arrange the muffin halves in the dish, cut side up, cutting as needed to fill spaces. Sprinkle with I cup of cheese, followed by the asparagus, bacon, and bell pepper. In a medium bowl, whisk the eggs, milk, mustard, salt, and pepper until combined; pour evenly over asparagus. Refrigerate, covered, for at least 4 hours or overnight.

Preheat oven to 375 degrees. Sprinkle casserole with remaining cheese. Bake, uncovered, 40–45 minutes, or until a knife inserted near the center comes out clean. Cool dish on wire rack for 5 minutes before cutting. Makes 8 servings.

APPETIZERS

BACON, JALAPENO, AND CORN CON QUESO DIP

8 strips	**bacon**
1 tablespoon	**butter**
2 1/2 cups	**fresh or frozen corn kernels,** thawed
1	**jalapeno,** seeded and minced
8 ounces	**cream cheese,** softened
1 cup	**grated mozzarella cheese**
1/2 teaspoon	**salt**
1/8 teaspoon	**cayenne pepper**
	tortilla chips

Preheat oven to 400 degrees.

In a large cast iron or oven-proof frying pan, cook the bacon over medium heat until lightly browned. Transfer bacon to paper towels to drain; crumble and reserve.

Discard all but 1 teaspoon of pan drippings. Return pan to heat and add the butter; cook over medium heat until melted. Add the corn and cook, stirring frequently, until cooked through, 4–5 minutes. Add the jalapeno and cook for another 2 minutes.

Remove from heat and add the cream cheese, stirring until blended. Add the mozzarella cheese, salt, cayenne pepper, and bacon, and stir to combine. Bake, uncovered, until mixture is hot and bubbly, about 20 minutes. Remove from oven, cool for 5 minutes, and serve warm with tortilla chips. Makes 8 servings.

CRISPY BACON TAQUITOS

¹/₂ cup	**grated cheddar cheese**
2 tablespoons	**cream cheese,** softened
2 tablespoons	**salsa**
6 strips	**bacon,** cooked and crumbled
I cup	**finely chopped cooked chicken**
¹/₂ teaspoon	**pepper**
¹/₄ teaspoon	**cumin**
¹/₄ teaspoon	**salt**
12	**corn tortillas**
I cup	**guacamole**

Preheat oven to 350 degrees. Lightly prepare a large baking sheet with nonstick cooking spray.

In a medium bowl, combine the cheese, cream cheese, and salsa; stir until blended. Add the bacon, chicken, pepper, cumin, and salt; stir until combined.

Heat a frying pan over medium heat and warm I tortilla until flexible, about 10 seconds per side. Spread I heaping tablespoon of chicken mixture evenly over tortilla and roll to make a tight cylinder. Arrange seam side down on prepared baking sheet. Repeat with the remaining tortillas and filling. Bake for 15 minutes, remove from oven and turn taquitos over for even browning. Return to oven and continue baking until taquitos are crispy and browned, about 15 more minutes. Serve with guacamole. Makes 12 servings.

CHEESY BACON RANCH BREAD BITES

1	**whole round loaf sourdough bread**
3 cups	**grated cheddar cheese**
6 strips	**bacon,** cooked and crumbled
1/2 cup	**butter,** melted
1 tablespoon	**ranch dressing mix**

Preheat oven to 350 degrees. Cut a length of aluminum foil long enough to wrap around the bread and spray lightly with cooking spray; reserve.

Use a sharp serrated knife to cut the loaf in 1-inch strips without cutting through the bottom crust. Turn bread 90 degrees and cut crosswise in 1-inch strips without cutting through bottom crust. Transfer bread to the center of the aluminum foil, pull the bread strips apart gently, and sprinkle cheese between each of the bread strips. Repeat this process with the crumbled bacon.

In a small bowl, combine the butter with ranch dressing mix and whisk to combine. Drizzle mixture evenly over bread. Wrap the aluminum foil around the bread, transfer to a baking sheet, and bake for 15 minutes. Pull foil back from top of bread and continue baking until cheese is completely melted, about 10 more minutes. Makes 6 servings.

BACON-WRAPPED BEER BRATS

4	**bratwurst sausages**
I can or bottle (12 ounces)	**regular or non-alcoholic beer**
6 tablespoons	**brown sugar**
1/2 teaspoon	**pepper**
1/4 teaspoon	**cayenne pepper**
8 strips	**bacon,** cut in half

Poke sausages several times with a small fork and arrange in a medium frying pan over high heat. Pour the beer around the sausages and bring to a boil. Reduce heat to low, cover and simmer for 15 minutes. Remove sausages to paper towels to drain. Discard beer.

Preheat oven to 425 degrees. Line a baking sheet with aluminum foil and place a wire rack on top; reserve.

In a medium bowl, combine the brown sugar, pepper, and cayenne pepper; reserve. Cut each bratwurst into 4 even pieces, wrap each piece with half strip of bacon, and secure with a toothpick. Toss the bratwurst in the brown sugar mixture to coat and place on prepared baking sheet. Bake, turning once, until the bacon is brown and crisp, about 25–35 minutes. Makes 8 servings.

SLOW COOKER BACON CHEESEBURGER DIP

1 pound	**lean ground beef**
2 cups	**grated cheddar cheese**
8 ounces	**cream cheese,** softened
1 can (10 ounces)	**diced tomatoes with green chiles,** with liquid
1 pound	**bacon,** cooked and crumbled
1 tablespoon	**finely chopped flat-leaf parsley** **scoop-style corn chips**

In a large frying pan over medium heat, cook the ground beef, stirring occasionally, until browned. Drain, discard excess grease, and wipe out the pan; return to heat. Return ground beef to pan and add the cheese, cream cheese, and tomatoes. Cook, stirring frequently until everything is heated through and well blended.

Pour mixture into a 2-quart slow cooker. Cover and cook on low for 2 hours, stirring occasionally. Add the bacon and heat for 1 more hour, stirring occasionally. Stir in parsley and serve with corn chips. Makes 6 servings.

BAKED BRIE WITH CANDIED BACON

$1/2$ pound	**bacon,** diced
$1/4$ cup	**dark brown sugar**
I tablespoon	**balsamic vinegar**
I tablespoon	**maple syrup**
$1/8$ teaspoon	**pepper**
I round (8 ounces)	**Brie cheese**
	assorted crackers

Preheat oven to 350 degrees. Line a baking sheet with aluminum foil and spray lightly with nonstick cooking spray.

In a large frying pan over medium heat, cook the bacon until lightly browned, stirring frequently. Transfer bacon to paper towels to drain, and discard pan drippings; do not wipe out pan. Return pan to heat and add back the bacon, brown sugar, vinegar, maple syrup, and pepper. Cook, stirring, until mixture comes to a simmer, about 2–3 minutes. Remove from heat and reserve.

Place Brie in the center of prepared baking sheet and top with bacon mixture. Bake until warm, about 10–12 minutes. Remove from oven and transfer to a serving dish. Serve warm with crackers. Makes 6 servings.

CARAMELIZED ONION AND BACON DIP

2	**large onions**
2 tablespoons	**olive oil**
2 cloves	**garlic,** peeled and minced
8 ounces	**cream cheese,** softened
I cup	**sour cream**
8 strips	**bacon,** cooked and crumbled
	salt and pepper, to taste
	potato chips

Peel and quarter the onions, and cut each quarter in ¼-inch strips. Heat the olive oil in a large frying pan over medium heat. Add the onions and cook, stirring frequently, until transparent, about 6 minutes. Lower the heat to medium-low, cover and cook, stirring occasionally, until onions are medium brown and caramelized, about 30–35 minutes. Add the garlic and cook for 2 minutes. Remove from heat.

In a medium bowl combine the cream cheese and sour cream; stir until well blended. Add the caramelized onions and bacon and stir until well combined. Season with salt and pepper. Serve with potato chips. Makes 8 servings.

BACON BATONS

I pound	**sliced bacon**
$^1/_3$ cup	**packed light brown sugar**
I $^1/_2$ tablespoons	**chili powder**
2 packages (3 ounces each)	**thin, grissini-style bread sticks**

Preheat oven to 325 degrees. Line a baking sheet with aluminum foil. Place a wire rack on top and reserve.

Cut each bacon strip in half lengthwise to make a long, skinny strip and arrange on a work surface. In a small dish, combine the brown sugar and chili powder. Sprinkle both sides of each bacon strip with the sugar mixture, pressing with fingers to coat if necessary.

Spiral wrap the bacon strips tightly around the bread sticks and arrange on the rack of the prepared pan. Bake until bacon is brown and crispy, about 18–20 minutes, checking frequently to make sure batons don't burn. Remove from the oven and cool for 30 minutes. Makes about 24 batons.

BACON CRAB DIP

6 strips	**bacon,** chopped
3	**green onions,** chopped
1	**red bell pepper,** seeds removed and finely chopped
8 ounces	**cream cheese,** softened
1/2 pound	**crab meat,** picked over for shells
1/4 cup	**cream**
1/2 teaspoon	**lemon pepper seasoning**
1/4 teaspoon	**Cajun seasoning**
1/2 cup	**panko crumbs**
1/2 teaspoon	**paprika**
	assorted crackers

Preheat oven to 400 degrees. Lightly spray a 1-quart baking dish with nonstick cooking spray.

In a large frying pan over medium heat, cook the bacon until lightly browned, stirring frequently. Transfer bacon to paper towels to drain, and reserve. Discard all but 1 tablespoon of pan drippings.

Return the pan to heat and add the onions and bell pepper. Cook over medium heat, stirring often, until tender, about 5 minutes. Add the cream cheese and cook until melted. Add the crab, cream, lemon pepper, Cajun seasoning, and bacon, and stir gently to combine. Transfer to the prepared dish. Evenly sprinkle the panko crumbs and paprika over the top. Bake until mixture bubbles and is lightly browned, about 30 minutes. Serve with crackers. Makes 8 servings.

BACON CHEESE FRIES

I package (32 ounces)	**frozen French fried potatoes**
	salt and pepper, to taste
I cup	**grated cheddar cheese**
4	**green onions,** thinly sliced
8 strips	**bacon,** cooked and crumbled
I cup	**ranch salad dressing**

Cook French fries according to package directions and sprinkle with salt and pepper.

Preheat the oven broiler and arrange fries in a broiler-proof baking pan or dish. Top evenly with cheese, onions, and bacon. Broil until cheese is melted, about 1–2 minutes. Serve with ranch dressing. Makes 8 servings.

BACON GUACAMOLE

4	**ripe avocados,** peeled and halved
I	**lime,** juiced
I tablespoon	**salsa**
I teaspoon	**minced garlic**
1/2 teaspoon	**salt**
1/2 teaspoon	**pepper**
1/4 cup	**finely diced red onion**
I large	**tomato,** seeded and finely diced
8 strips	**bacon,** cooked and finely crumbled
3 tablespoons	**chopped fresh cilantro**
	tortilla chips

In a medium bowl, mash the avocados with the lime juice, salsa, garlic, salt, and pepper. Add the onion, tomato, bacon, and cilantro, and stir gently just until blended. Serve at once with tortilla chips. Makes 8 servings.

APRICOT DEVILS ON HORSEBACK

12 strips	**bacon,** cut in half
1 bag (6 ounces)	**dried apricots**
$^1/_2$ cup	**barbecue sauce**
1 tablespoon	**maple syrup**
1 $^1/_2$ teaspoons	**prepared mustard**

Preheat oven to 350 degrees. Line a large baking sheet with aluminum foil.

In a large frying pan, cook bacon over medium heat until partially cooked but not crisp. Transfer bacon to paper towels to drain. Wrap 1 bacon piece around each apricot and secure with a toothpick. Arrange on prepared baking sheet. Bake until bacon is crisp, about 15–18 minutes.

In a small bowl, combine the barbecue sauce, maple syrup, and mustard; stir to blend. Remove pan from oven and serve with sauce for dipping. Makes about 24 appetizers.

BACON MINI QUESADILLAS

10 (8-inch)	**flour tortillas**
1 1/2 cups	**grated cheddar cheese**
4 ounces	**cream cheese,** softened
1 1/4 cups	**finely chopped cooked chicken**
6 strips	**bacon,** cooked and finely crumbled
1	**large Anaheim pepper,** seeded and chopped fine
1/4 teaspoon	**pepper**
3 tablespoons	**butter,** melted
	salt
1/2 cup	**salsa**
1/2 cup	**sour cream**

Preheat oven to 375 degrees. Line a large baking sheet with aluminum foil. Using a round 2-inch biscuit cutter, cut 5 rounds from each tortilla (50 rounds total); reserve.

In a medium bowl, combine the cheese and cream cheese; stir to blend. Add the chicken, bacon, chopped pepper, and pepper, and stir until combined. Brush half of the tortilla rounds with melted butter and arrange butter side down on prepared baking sheet. Top each with about 1 heaping tablespoon of chicken mixture. Top with remaining tortilla rounds, brush with butter, and sprinkle with salt. Bake until quesadillas are lightly browned, about 15 minutes.

In a small bowl, combine salsa and sour cream and stir to blend. Remove quesadillas from oven and cool on pan for 5 minutes before transferring to a serving platter. Serve with sour cream mixture for dipping. Makes 25 appetizers.

ULTIMATE SPINACH DIP

6 strips	**bacon**
1/2 pound	**fresh spinach,** stems removed and chopped
2 cloves	**garlic,** peeled and minced
8 ounces	**cream cheese,** softened
1/2 cup	**sour cream**
1/4 cup	**grated Parmesan cheese**
2 teaspoons	**lemon juice**
I tablespoon	**chopped flat-leaf parsley**
	salt and pepper, to taste
	assorted crackers

Preheat oven to 350 degrees. Prepare a 16-ounce souffle or baking dish with nonstick cooking spray.

In a large frying pan, cook bacon over medium heat until crispy. Transfer bacon to paper towels to drain, and discard all but 2 tablespoons of pan drippings. Return pan to heat and add the spinach and garlic. Cook over medium heat, stirring frequently, until spinach wilts and garlic is fragrant, about 1–2 minutes. Crumble the bacon and add to spinach mixture; stir to combine.

In a medium bowl, combine the cream cheese, sour cream, Parmesan, and lemon juice; stir to blend. Add the spinach mixture and stir until combined. Season with salt and pepper. Transfer to prepared baking dish and smooth top. Bake until mixture bubbles and top is lightly browned, about 25 minutes. Sprinkle with parsley and serve with crackers. Makes 6 servings.

BACON CREAM CHEESE CHICKEN BITES

4 strips	**bacon**
4	**boneless, skinless chicken breasts**
8 ounces	**cream cheese,** softened
$1/4$ cup	**chopped green onions**
	salt and pepper, to taste

Preheat oven to 375 degrees. Line a baking sheet with aluminum foil or parchment paper.

In a large frying pan, cook bacon over medium heat until it just starts to brown. Transfer bacon to paper towels to drain; reserve.

Flatten the chicken by pounding it to a $1/4$-inch thickness and pat dry with paper towels. In a small bowl, combine the cream cheese and onions; stir until blended. Spread each chicken breast with $1/4$ of the mixture and sprinkle with salt and pepper.

Roll each chicken breast up jelly roll style and spiral wrap with a piece of bacon, securing ends with toothpicks. Arrange the chicken rolls on the prepared baking sheet and bake, turning once, until chicken is cooked through and bacon is brown and crispy, about 30 minutes. Remove from oven and cool chicken on the pan for 10 minutes. Use a sharp knife to carefully cut each roll into 6 pieces and transfer to a serving platter. Serve with toothpicks. Makes 24 appetizers.

BACON-WRAPPED STUFFING WITH CRANBERRY DIPPING SAUCE

2 cups	**prepared or leftover stuffing**
8 strips	**bacon**
$1/2$ cup	**jellied cranberry sauce**
1 $1/2$ tablespoons	**stone-ground mustard**
1 tablespoon	**brown sugar**

Preheat oven to 375 degrees. Line a baking sheet with parchment.

Using a tablespoon, roll stuffing into 16 balls. Cut each strip of bacon in half widthwise. Wrap each stuffing ball with a piece of bacon and secure with a toothpick. Arrange on prepared baking sheet, seam side down. Bake until bacon is brown and crispy, turning once halfway through cooking, about 30 minutes.

Combine the cranberry sauce, mustard, and brown sugar in a small bowl and whisk until smooth. Serve appetizers warm with dipping sauce. Makes 16 appetizers.

BACON SPUDLETS

6	**medium red potatoes**
I teaspoon	**canola oil**
$^1/_4$ teaspoon	**seasoning salt**
$^1/_4$ teaspoon	**garlic powder**
	salt and pepper
12 strips	**bacon,** cut in half
$^3/_4$ cup	**sour cream**
I teaspoon	**hot pepper sauce**

Preheat oven to 425 degrees. Line a large baking sheet with parchment paper or aluminum foil. Lightly spray a broiling rack with nonstick cooking spray and place it on top of the baking sheet.

Cut each potato in 4 wedges. Place the wedges in a large bowl and drizzle with oil. Sprinkle with seasoning salt, garlic powder, and a pinch of salt and pepper. Toss until the potatoes are evenly coated.

Wrap each potato wedge with a half strip of bacon, secure with toothpicks, and arrange on the prepared pan. Bake until bacon is crispy and potatoes are tender, turning once during cooking, about 30–35 minutes. Remove from oven and cool for 5 minutes.

In a small bowl, combine the sour cream and hot sauce and stir to blend. Season to taste with salt and pepper. Serve the dipping sauce with warm spudlets. Makes 24 appetizers.

JALAPENO BACON RANGOONS

1/2 pound	**bacon,** diced
3	**medium jalapenos,** seeded and minced
8 ounces	**cream cheese,** softened
1 tablespoon	**milk**
1/4 teaspoon	**garlic powder**
24	**wonton wrappers**
	peanut oil
	salt
2/3 cup	**sweet and sour sauce**

In a large frying pan, cook bacon over medium heat until lightly browned. Transfer bacon to paper towels to drain, and discard all but 2 teaspoons of pan drippings. Return pan to heat and cook the jalapenos over medium heat, stirring frequently, until tender, 3–4 minutes. Remove from heat and reserve.

In a medium bowl, mix together the cream cheese, milk, and garlic powder until well blended. Add the reserved bacon and jalapenos, and stir to combine. Spoon 1 tablespoon of the mixture in the middle of a wonton wrapper. Moisten the outer edges of the wrapper with a little bit of water and bring the 4 points together in the center, pinching seams tightly to seal. Repeat with remaining wrappers and filling.

In a deep fryer or heavy pot, heat 2 inches of oil over medium heat to 365 degrees. Fry the rangoons a few at a time, turning once, until golden brown and crispy, about 1–2 minutes per side. Drain on paper towels, sprinkle with salt, and serve with sweet and sour sauce. Makes 24 rangoons.

SOUPS

BACON AND CHICKEN WILD RICE CHOWDER

7 cups	**chicken stock or broth**
2 1/2 cups	**chopped cooked chicken**
1 cup	**uncooked wild rice**
1/2 cup	**chopped onion**
2 stalks	**celery,** diced
2	**large carrots,** peeled and diced
4 cups	**grated sharp cheddar cheese,** divided
1 cup	**heavy cream**
8 strips	**bacon,** cooked and finely crumbled
	salt and pepper, to taste
1/4 cup	**chopped green onions**

Prepare a 4-quart slow cooker with nonstick cooking spray. Add chicken stock, chicken, wild rice, onion, celery, and carrots; stir to combine. Cover and cook on low heat for 7–8 hours.

Stir in 3 cups of cheese, cream, and bacon. Continue to cook, stirring occasionally, until cheese is melted and mixture is creamy. Top with remaining 1 cup cheese and chopped green onions. Makes 8 servings.

BACON TOMATO BISQUE

6 strips	**bacon,** finely chopped
I	**large onion,** chopped
I	**carrot,** peeled and chopped
I stalk	**celery,** chopped
2 cloves	**garlic,** peeled and finely chopped
5 tablespoons	**flour**
4$^1/_2$ cups	**low-sodium chicken stock or broth**
I can (28 ounces)	**whole Italian tomatoes,** peeled
$^1/_4$ teaspoon	**baking soda**
$^1/_2$ tablespoon	**chopped flat-leaf parsley**
$^1/_2$ teaspoon	**chopped fresh thyme leaves**
I	**bay leaf**
I cup	**heavy cream**
I teaspoon	**salt**
$^1/_2$ teaspoon	**pepper**

In a Dutch oven or large, heavy pot, cook the bacon over medium heat until lightly browned. Transfer bacon to paper towels to drain, and discard all but I tablespoon of pan drippings. Return pot to heat and add the onion, carrot, celery, and garlic. Cook, stirring occasionally, until carrots are tender, about 8 minutes. Add the flour and cook, stirring, for 3 minutes. Pour in the chicken stock and stir until smooth. Chop the tomatoes, discarding the cores, and add to the pot along with the juice from the can; add the baking soda and stir. Heat, stirring constantly, until mixture comes to a boil. Add the parsley, thyme, and bay leaf and lower the heat to medium-low; simmer for 20 minutes. Remove the bay leaf.

Use an immersion blender to puree the mixture. (Alternately, working in batches, transfer the mixture to a blender or food processor and puree until smooth. Return the puree to the pot and reheat over medium heat.) Whisk in cream, salt, pepper, and reserved bacon, and heat for 2 minutes before serving. Makes 6 servings.

ROASTED GARLIC, BACON, AND POTATO SOUP

2	**whole heads garlic**
3 tablespoons	**butter,** melted, divided
2 pounds	**potatoes,** peeled and cut in 1-inch cubes
2	**medium onions,** quartered
2 tablespoons	**olive oil**
$1/2$ teaspoon	**salt**
$1/4$ teaspoon	**pepper**
6 cups	**low-sodium chicken stock or broth,** divided
$4 1/2$ teaspoons	**flour**
$1/2$	**cup milk**
8 strips	**bacon,** cooked and crumbled

Preheat oven to 400 degrees. Remove papery outer skin from garlic, keeping heads intact. Cut about $1/2$ inch off the top, revealing just the top of the bulbs. Place in the center of a 9 x 13-inch baking dish and drizzle with 1 tablespoon melted butter.

In a large bowl, combine the potatoes and onions. Drizzle with oil and sprinkle with salt and pepper, tossing to coat. Spoon the mixture in a single layer around the garlic and cover with foil. Bake until potatoes are tender, stirring occasionally, about 40 minutes. Remove from oven and cool for 10 minutes. Squeeze the softened garlic on top of the potato mixture. Working in batches, puree the potato-garlic mixture with 4 cups chicken stock until smooth; reserve. In a large saucepan over medium heat, heat remaining 2 tablespoons melted butter and whisk in flour until smooth; gradually add 2 cups chicken stock. Bring to a boil; cook and stir until thickened, about 2 minutes. Stir in milk and potato puree and heat through. Sprinkle with crumbled bacon and serve. Makes 8 servings.

BACON CHEESEBURGER BREWSKI SOUP

I pound	**lean ground beef**
I package (12 ounces)	**lean center-cut bacon,** chopped
I	**onion,** diced
2 cloves	**garlic,** peeled and chopped
1/4 cup	**flour**
3 cups	**beef stock or broth**
I can or bottle (12 ounces)	**beer**
I teaspoon	**paprika**
1/2 teaspoon	**salt**
1/2 teaspoon	**pepper**
2 cups	**half-and-half**
4 cups	**grated mild cheddar cheese**
2	**hamburger buns,** cut in 1-inch cubes and toasted
8	**sandwich-style pickle slices,** cut in 1/2-inch pieces

In a Dutch oven or large, heavy pot, cook the ground beef over medium heat, breaking up meat with a spoon, until lightly browned and no longer pink. Transfer meat to paper towels to drain. Reserve. Wipe out pot and return to heat. Cook the bacon, stirring occasionally, until lightly browned, about 5 minutes. Transfer bacon to paper towels to drain, and discard all but 2 tablespoons of pan drippings; return pot to heat. Add the onion and cook until tender, about 4–5 minutes. Add the garlic and cook until fragrant, about 1 minute. Stir in the flour and cook until lightly browned, about 2 minutes. Add the beef stock, beer, paprika, salt, pepper, beef, and bacon, and cook over medium heat until mixture just comes to a boil. Reduce heat and simmer for 15 minutes. Add the half-and-half and cheese, and cook on medium-low until the cheese has melted. Serve garnished with the croutons and pickles. Makes 8 servings.

ITALIAN TORTELLINI SOUP

I tablespoon	**olive oil**
6 strips	**bacon,** finely diced
I	**medium onion,** finely chopped
3 cloves	**garlic,** peeled and minced
I can (28 ounces)	**whole Italian tomatoes,** with liquid
6 cups	**low-sodium chicken stock or broth**
2 teaspoons	**Italian seasoning**
I package (9 ounces)	**refrigerated cheese tortellini**
$^1/_2$ pound	**fresh spinach,** chopped
	salt and pepper, to taste
$^1/_2$ cup	**grated fresh Parmesan cheese**

In a Dutch oven or large, heavy pot, heat the oil over medium heat and add the bacon, cooking until lightly browned. Drain all but I tablespoon of pan drippings; return pot to heat. Add the onion and cook until tender, about 4 minutes. Add the garlic and continue cooking until fragrant, about I more minute. Chop the tomatoes, removing cores, and add to the pot along with the juice from the can. Add chicken stock and Italian seasoning and heat to simmering.

Bring a large pot of water to a boil over medium-high heat and cook tortellini according to package directions. Drain, and add hot tortellini to soup mixture. Add the spinach and cook just until wilted, about I minute. Season with salt and pepper and top with Parmesan cheese before serving. Makes 8 servings.

CREAM OF ASPARAGUS AND BACON SOUP

6 strips	**bacon,** chopped
1 large	**onion,** chopped
2 pounds	**asparagus,** cut in 2-inch pieces
5–6 cups	**chicken stock or broth,** divided
1/2 cup	**heavy cream**
1/4 teaspoon	**lemon juice**
	salt and pepper, to taste

In a Dutch oven or large, heavy pot, cook the bacon over medium heat until it starts to crisp, about 6–8 minutes. Transfer bacon to paper towels to drain, and discard all but 2 tablespoons of pan drippings; return pot to heat. Cook the onion, stirring often, until translucent, about 5 minutes. Add asparagus and cook, stirring, for 5 minutes. Add 5 cups chicken stock and simmer, covered, until asparagus is very tender, 15–20 minutes.

Puree soup in batches in a food processor or blender until smooth. Return pan to heat, and stir in cream until combined. If necessary, add more chicken stock to thin soup to desired consistency. Add lemon juice, season with salt and pepper, and bring soup to a simmer. Remove from heat and serve with bacon sprinkled on top. Makes 6 servings.

FRENCH ONION AND BACON SOUP

8 strips	**bacon,** chopped
2	**large onions,** thinly sliced, separated into rings
5 cups	**beef stock or broth**
1/2 teaspoon	**pepper**
1/4 teaspoon	**dried thyme**
1/4 teaspoon	**garlic powder**
6 slices	**French bread,** toasted
1 cup	**grated Swiss cheese**
3 tablespoons	**grated fresh Parmesan cheese**

In a Dutch oven or large, heavy pot, cook the bacon over medium heat, stirring, until lightly browned. Transfer bacon to paper towels to drain, and discard all but 2 tablespoons of pan drippings. Return pot to heat and add the onions. Cook, stirring frequently, until onions are browned and starting to caramelize, about 30 minutes. Add the beef stock, pepper, thyme, and garlic powder and bring to a boil. Reduce heat and simmer for 15 minutes. Stir in reserved bacon and remove from heat.

Heat oven broiler. Ladle soup into 6 ovenproof bowls and place 1 slice of bread in each bowl. Sprinkle Swiss and Parmesan cheeses evenly over top and broil, 4 inches from heat, until cheeses are melted and starting to brown, about 2 minutes. Makes 6 servings.

FRENCH LENTIL BACON VEGETABLE SOUP

4 strips	**lean bacon,** finely chopped
I	**large yellow onion,** finely chopped
2 stalks	**celery,** finely chopped
2	**medium carrots,** peeled and diced
2 cloves	**garlic,** peeled and minced
I can (14.5 ounces)	**diced tomatoes,** with liquid
6 cups	**chicken stock or broth**
I cup	**French lentils**
1/2 teaspoon	**dried thyme**
2	**bay leaves**
I teaspoon	**salt**
1/4 teaspoon	**freshly ground black pepper**
2 tablespoons	**chopped flat-leaf parsley**

In a Dutch oven or large, heavy pot, cook the bacon over medium heat, stirring frequently, until lightly browned, 4–5 minutes. Add the onion and celery, and cook, stirring occasionally, until soft and translucent, about 5 minutes. Add the carrots and garlic, stirring constantly, and cook I minute more. Add the tomatoes and juice from the can, chicken stock, lentils, thyme, bay leaves, salt, and pepper, and bring to a boil. Cover, reduce heat to low, and simmer until the lentils are tender, about 30–45 minutes. Remove bay leaves, and garnish with parsley before serving. Makes 8 servings.

CREAMY CAULIFLOWER BACON SOUP

1/2 pound	**bacon,** chopped
1	**medium onion,** chopped
1 head (2 1/2 pounds)	**cauliflower,** cored and chopped in florets
3 cups	**chicken stock or broth**
4 ounces	**cream cheese,** softened
1/2 cup	**heavy cream**
1 tablespoon	**chopped fresh chives**
	salt and pepper, to taste
1/2 cup	**grated cheddar cheese**

In a large saucepan over medium heat, cook bacon until crisp. Transfer bacon to paper towels to drain, and discard all but 1 tablespoon of pan drippings; return pan to heat.

Add onion and cook over medium heat, stirring occasionally, until translucent and just starting to brown, about 8 minutes. Add the cauliflower and chicken stock and increase heat to medium-high. Cook, stirring occasionally, until mixture boils. Reduce heat, cover and simmer until cauliflower is very tender, 15–20 minutes.

Add the cream cheese and stir until it melts. Use an immersion blender, pulsing several times, or a potato masher to lightly mash the cauliflower. Stir in the cream, chives, and all but 2 tablespoons of the bacon; season with salt and pepper. Serve garnished with grated cheese and reserved bacon. Makes 6 servings.

BUTTERNUT SQUASH AND BACON SOUP

1	**butternut squash** (about 3 pounds), peeled, seeded, and cut in 1-inch chunks
1	**onion,** diced
1	**red bell pepper,** seeds removed and chopped
2 tablespoons	**olive oil**
2 cloves	**garlic,** peeled and minced
	salt and pepper, to taste
1/2 teaspoon	**dried thyme**
3–4 cups	**chicken stock or broth,** divided
8 strips	**bacon,** cooked and crumbled
1 tablespoon	**chopped fresh chives**

Preheat oven to 400 degrees. Lightly spray a baking sheet with nonstick cooking spray. Arrange squash, onion, and bell pepper in a single layer on prepared baking sheet. Drizzle with olive oil, and add the garlic, salt, and pepper. Gently toss to combine. Bake, stirring once or twice, until squash is tender, about 25–30 minutes.

Heat a Dutch oven or large, heavy pot over medium heat. Add squash mixture and thyme, and cook, stirring occasionally, until fragrant, about 1–2 minutes. Stir in 3 cups chicken stock and puree with an immersion blender. (Alternately, working in batches, transfer the mixture to a blender or food processor and puree until smooth. Return the puree to the pot and reheat over medium heat.) Bring to a boil; reduce heat, and simmer until slightly thickened, about 10 minutes. Add more chicken stock, if needed, until soup is desired consistency. Adjust seasonings if necessary. Add bacon and heat until mixture starts to simmer. Serve immediately, garnished with chives. Makes 6 servings.

BACON BROCCOLI CHEDDAR SOUP

3 cups	**chicken stock or broth**
2	**large carrots,** peeled and diced
4 stalks	**celery,** diced
2	**large potatoes,** peeled and diced
I	**onion,** finely chopped
I	**large head broccoli** (about 2 pounds), cored and chopped in florets
3 tablespoons	**butter**
$^1/_3$ cup	**flour**
3 cups	**milk**
4 cups	**grated sharp cheddar cheese**
I teaspoon	**salt**
$^1/_2$ teaspoon	**pepper**
I teaspoon	**dry mustard**
6 strips	**bacon,** cooked and crumbled

In a Dutch oven or large, heavy pot, combine the chicken stock, carrots, celery, potatoes, and onion. Bring mixture to a boil, cover and simmer until the vegetables are tender, about 10–12 minutes. Add the chopped broccoli. Cover and simmer for another 10 minutes.

Melt the butter in a medium saucepan over medium heat. Whisk in the flour and cook, stirring constantly, until lightly browned, 1–2 minutes. Gradually whisk in the milk and cook until the mixture is bubbling and slightly thickened, 5–7 minutes. Add the cheese one handful at a time and whisk until melted and fully incorporated into the mixture. Stir in the salt, pepper, and mustard. Slowly stir the cheese mixture into the vegetables until well combined. Stir in the bacon and adjust seasonings, if necessary. Makes 6 servings.

BACON, WHITE BEAN, AND KALE SOUP

8 strips	**bacon,** chopped
I	**medium onion,** finely chopped
2 cloves	**garlic,** peeled and finely chopped
I	**medium carrot,** peeled and chopped
2 stalks	**celery,** chopped
6 cups	**chicken stock or broth**
4 cups	**chopped kale leaves**
2 cans (15 ounces each)	**white beans,** rinsed and drained
I can (14.5 ounces)	**diced tomatoes,** with liquid
1/2 teaspoon	**minced fresh thyme**
	salt and pepper, to taste
1/2 cup	**grated Parmesan cheese**

In a Dutch oven or large, heavy pot, cook bacon over medium heat until crisp. Transfer bacon to paper towels to drain, and discard all but I tablespoon of pan drippings.

Return pot to heat and add the onion. Cook, stirring occasionally, until translucent, about 5 minutes. Add the garlic, carrot, and celery, and continue cooking until carrot is tender, about 5 minutes. Add the chicken stock, kale, beans, tomatoes, thyme, and reserved bacon. Cook, stirring occasionally, until mixture comes to a boil. Reduce heat, cover, and simmer until kale is tender, about 15 minutes. Season with salt and pepper and serve topped with Parmesan cheese. Makes 8 servings.

SALADS

CHINESE CRUNCH SALAD

1/4 cup	**creamy peanut butter**
2 tablespoons	**rice vinegar**
2 tablespoons	**lime juice**
3 tablespoons	**vegetable oil**
I tablespoon	**soy sauce**
2 tablespoons	**honey**
2 1/2 tablespoons	**sugar**
2 cloves	**garlic,** peeled and minced
I-inch piece	**fresh ginger,** peeled and minced
I teaspoon	**salt**
1/4 cup	**chopped fresh cilantro,** divided
4 cups	**coleslaw mix**
2	**large carrots,** peeled and shredded
I	**red bell pepper,** seeds removed and finely chopped
I	**small English cucumber,** halved lengthwise, seeded and thinly sliced
I cup	**frozen or fresh shelled edamame,** cooked and cooled
8 strips	**bacon,** cooked and crumbled
3/4 cup	**crispy chow mein noodles**

Combine the peanut butter, vinegar, lime juice, oil, soy sauce, honey, sugar, garlic, ginger, and salt in a food processor or blender, and process until completely smooth. Add half of the cilantro and pulse just until the cilantro is finely chopped. Refrigerate dressing, tightly covered, until ready to serve. In a large bowl, combine the coleslaw mix, carrots, bell pepper, cucumber, and edamame; toss to combine. Drizzle with the peanut dressing and toss to coat evenly. Sprinkle with the crumbled bacon, chow mein noodles, and remaining cilantro, and toss gently. Makes 6 servings.

WARM BACON AND CHICKEN RANCH SALAD

8 strips	**bacon,** chopped
I pound	**boneless, skinless chicken breasts,** cut in I-inch pieces
$^1/_2$ teaspoon	**paprika**
$^1/_4$ teaspoon	**salt**
$^1/_4$ teaspoon	**pepper**
$^1/_4$ teaspoon	**garlic powder**
I pound	**fresh baby spinach,** stems removed
2 cups	**halved grape tomatoes**
$^1/_4$	**red onion,** sliced
I cup	**grated mild cheddar cheese**
I	**large English cucumber,** sliced
I cup	**ranch salad dressing**

Cook the bacon in a large frying pan over medium heat until browned and crispy. Transfer bacon to paper towels to drain, and discard all but I tablespoon of pan drippings.

Return pan to heat, add the chicken and cook, stirring occasionally, until chicken is cooked through and lightly browned, about 10 minutes. Sprinkle with paprika, salt, pepper, and garlic powder, and stir to coat. Remove from heat, cover, and reserve.

In a large bowl, combine the spinach, tomatoes, onion, cheese, and cucumber. Drizzle with the dressing and toss gently. Divide the salad evenly among 6 chilled salad plates and top with the warm chicken. Sprinkle reserved bacon on top and serve. Makes 6 servings.

CREAMY AVOCADO, BACON, AND SWEET CORN SALAD

6 strips	**thick-cut bacon**
6	**large ears corn,** husks and silks removed
3	**avocados,** peeled and diced
1/2 cup	**creamy Italian salad dressing**
1/2 cup	**crumbled feta cheese**
2 tablespoons	**chopped fresh cilantro**
	salt and freshly ground black pepper, to taste

Cook the bacon in a large frying pan over medium heat until browned and crispy. Transfer bacon to paper towels to drain, and discard all but 1 tablespoon of pan drippings.

Cut the corn kernels off the cobs and add to the frying pan with the bacon fat. Cook over medium-high heat, stirring frequently, until corn is tender and just starting to brown, about 5 minutes. Remove from heat and cool in the pan to room temperature. Crumble the bacon into the corn and toss to combine.

Transfer to a serving bowl and gently stir in the avocados. Drizzle in the salad dressing, and toss gently to combine. Sprinkle with the cheese, cilantro, salt, and pepper, and toss gently to combine. Makes 6 servings.

BROCCOLI AND BACON SALAD

I pound	**broccoli,** cut into florets
8 strips	**bacon,** cooked and crumbled
$^1/_2$	**small red onion,** chopped
$^1/_2$ cup	**grated mozzarella cheese**
$^1/_2$ cup	**grated Parmesan cheese**
$^1/_4$ cup	**sugar**
$^1/_2$ cup	**mayonnaise**
I tablespoon	**balsamic vinegar**

Place broccoli, bacon, onion, and cheeses in a salad bowl and toss gently.

In a small bowl, combine sugar, mayonnaise, and vinegar; stir until the sugar dissolves and mixture is smooth. Drizzle the dressing over the salad and toss gently to combine. Makes 6 servings.

GERMAN BACON SLAW

8 strips	**bacon,** chopped
I	**small red onion,** chopped
1/4 cup	**cider vinegar**
1/4 cup	**warm water**
2 tablespoons	**light brown sugar**
1/2 teaspoon	**celery seeds**
6 cups	**shredded cabbage**

Cook the bacon in a large frying pan over medium heat until browned and crispy. Transfer bacon to paper towels to drain, reserving pan drippings.

Return pan to heat, and cook the onion over medium heat until tender, about 5 minutes. Add the vinegar, water, brown sugar, and celery seeds and cook, stirring, until sugar dissolves. Add the cabbage and cook, stirring, until crisp-tender, about 5 minutes. Add the bacon and stir to combine. Serve warm. Makes 8 servings.

BEST BACON MACARONI SALAD

1 pound	**uncooked elbow macaroni**
1	**large tomato,** chopped
2 stalks	**celery,** chopped
3	**green onions,** finely chopped
1 cup	**mayonnaise**
$1/4$ cup	**ranch dressing**
1 tablespoon	**balsamic vinegar**
$1/4$ teaspoon	**salt**
$1/4$ teaspoon	**pepper**
1 cup	**grated sharp cheddar cheese**
1 pound	**bacon,** cooked and crumbled

Cook macaroni according to package directions; drain and rinse in cold water. Transfer to a large bowl; stir in tomato, celery, and green onions.

In a small bowl, whisk together the mayonnaise, ranch dressing, vinegar, salt, and pepper. Pour over macaroni and toss to coat. Refrigerate, covered, for at least 2 hours or overnight. Just before serving, mix in cheese and bacon. Makes 8 servings.

SPRING GREENS WITH APPLES, BACON, AND GORGONZOLA

1/2 cup	**olive oil**
3 tablespoons	**sugar**
3 tablespoons	**balsamic vinegar**
1/4 teaspoon	**salt**
1/8 teaspoon	**dry mustard**
1/8 teaspoon	**pepper**
6 cups	**spring mix salad greens**
6 strips	**bacon,** cooked and crumbled
2	**Granny Smith apples,** cored and chopped
1/2 cup	**dried cherries**
1/2 cup	**toasted sliced almonds**
1/4 cup	**Gorgonzola cheese,** crumbled

In a small bowl, whisk together the olive oil, sugar, vinegar, salt, mustard, and pepper.

In a large bowl, combine the greens, bacon, apples, cherries, almonds, and cheese. Drizzle the dressing over top and toss gently. To serve, divide the salad evenly among 6 chilled salad plates. Makes 6 servings.

PERFECT WEDGE SALAD

¹/₂ cup	**mayonnaise**
¹/₂ cup	**crumbled blue cheese,** divided
¹/₄ cup	**half-and-half**
1 tablespoon	**sour cream**
1¹/₂ teaspoons	**lemon juice**
¹/₄ teaspoon	**salt**
¹/₄ teaspoon	**pepper**
1	**large head iceberg lettuce**
1 pound	**bacon,** cooked and crumbled
16	**grape tomatoes,** quartered

In a medium bowl, whisk together the mayonnaise, ¹/₄ cup blue cheese, half-and-half, sour cream, lemon juice, salt, and pepper, until smooth.

Remove core from lettuce. Cut lettuce head in half, then cut each half into quarters. Place wedges on 8 chilled salad plates and drizzle with the dressing. Sprinkle with remaining ¹/₄ cup blue cheese, bacon, and tomatoes. Makes 8 servings.

WARM BACON POTATO SALAD WITH SOUR CREAM DRESSING

3 pounds	**small red potatoes,** quartered
2 tablespoons	**olive oil**
2	**shallots,** chopped
1 cup	**sour cream**
3/4 cup	**mayonnaise**
1 pound	**bacon,** cooked and crumbled
3	**green onions,** minced
1/2 teaspoon	**pepper**

Preheat oven to 350 degrees.

In a large bowl, combine potatoes with olive oil and toss to coat. Spread in a single layer on a baking sheet, and bake for 10 minutes. Remove pan from oven and sprinkle potatoes with shallots, stirring to mix. Return to oven and continue baking until potatoes are tender, about 10 more minutes.

In a large heatproof bowl, combine the sour cream, mayonnaise, bacon, green onions, and pepper; whisk until blended. When potatoes are done, remove from oven and carefully add to the sour cream mixture; stir to combine. Let rest at room temperature for 30 minutes, stirring occasionally to distribute dressing. Serve warm. Makes 8 servings.

WATERCRESS SALAD WITH BACON, CRAB, AND AVOCADO

6 cups	**watercress** (leaves and thin stems only)
1/2 pound	**jumbo lump crab,** drained and picked through for shells
2	**avocados,** peeled and diced
1/3 cup	**olive oil**
2 tablespoons	**fresh lime juice**
1/4 teaspoon	**salt**
1/4 teaspoon	**pepper**
1/2 pound	**bacon,** cooked and crumbled
1/3 cup	**pine nuts,** toasted

Divide the watercress among 6 chilled salad plates. Divide the crab among the plates and top with the avocados.

In a small bowl, whisk together the olive oil, lime juice, salt, and pepper. Drizzle the dressing over the salads and sprinkle with the bacon and pine nuts. Makes 6 servings.

SANDWICHES

BLEST SANDWICHES (BACON, LETTUCE, EGG SALAD, AND TOMATO)

6	**hard-cooked eggs,** peeled and chopped
1/4 cup	**mayonnaise**
2 tablespoons	**cream cheese,** softened
I teaspoon	**prepared mustard**
1/2 teaspoon	**onion powder**
1/4 teaspoon	**salt**
1/4 teaspoon	**pepper**
1/4 teaspoon	**Worcestershire sauce**
8 slices	**whole wheat bread,** toasted
4	**lettuce leaves**
4 slices	**tomato**
4 slices	**Swiss cheese**
8 strips	**bacon,** cooked

In a large bowl, combine the eggs, mayonnaise, cream cheese, mustard, onion powder, salt, pepper, and Worcestershire sauce.

On 4 slices of toast, layer the lettuce, tomato, and cheese slices. Cut the bacon strips in half and arrange 4 halves on each sandwich. Top with egg salad and remaining 4 slices of toast. Makes 4 servings.

BACON-WRAPPED CHEESE DOGS

8 strips	**bacon**
1	**small onion,** sliced
8	**hot dogs**
4 slices	**American cheese**
8	**hot dog buns,** toasted

In a large frying pan over medium heat, fry the bacon until lightly browned but still flexible. Transfer bacon to paper towels to drain, and discard all but 1 tablespoon of pan drippings. Return pan to heat and cook the onion, stirring often, until lightly browned, about 5–6 minutes; reserve.

Preheat oven to 450 degrees. Slice each hot dog lengthwise down the middle almost, but not all the way through. Cut the cheese slices in fourths and fill the pocket of each hot dog with 2 pieces of cheese.

Wrap each hot dog with a bacon strip, securing with toothpicks if necessary. Place hot dogs on a baking sheet and bake until cheese is melted and bacon and hot dogs are hot, about 10 minutes. Serve the dogs on the toasted buns topped with the onions. Makes 8 servings.

COBB CLUBS

¹/₃ cup	**mayonnaise**
I tablespoon	**crumbled blue cheese**
2 teaspoons	**minced fresh basil**
4	**croissants,** split
4	**lettuce leaves**
I	**medium tomato,** sliced
I	**avocado,** peeled and sliced
8 strips	**bacon,** cooked and halved
4 slices	**deli ham**
3	**hard-cooked eggs,** peeled and sliced

In a small bowl, combine the mayonnaise, blue cheese, and basil; spread over cut side of croissant tops and bottoms. Layer bottoms with lettuce, tomato, avocado, bacon, ham, and egg slices; replace tops. Makes 4 servings.

BACON CRAB MELTS

4 tablespoons	**mayonnaise**
I stalk	**celery,** finely chopped
I tablespoon	**lemon juice**
$1/2$ teaspoon	**seafood seasoning,** such as Old Bay
$1/2$ teaspoon	**Dijon mustard**
$1/8$ teaspoon	**salt**
$1/8$ teaspoon	**pepper**
12 ounces	**lump crabmeat,** drained and picked through for shells
4 tablespoons	**butter,** softened
8 slices	**sourdough bread**
8 thin slices	**cheddar cheese**
8 strips	**bacon,** cooked
2	**Roma tomatoes,** cut in $1/4$-inch slices

In a medium bowl, combine the mayonnaise, celery, lemon juice, seafood seasoning, mustard, salt, and pepper. Add the crabmeat and stir gently to combine.

Spread butter on 4 bread slices. Flip bread over and top each with I slice of cheese. Divide the crab mixture and spread over the cheese. Layer with bacon strips, tomatoes, and remaining cheese slices. Top with the remaining 4 bread slices. Spread the remaining butter on the tops of the sandwiches.

Heat a large frying pan over medium heat and cook the sandwiches, until both sides are golden brown and cheese has melted, about 3 minutes per side. Makes 4 servings.

BACON AND TURKEY GRILLED CHEESE

4 tablespoons	**butter,** softened, divided
1	**medium onion,** sliced
4 tablespoons	**barbecue sauce**
8 slices	**sourdough bread**
8 slices	**Monterey Jack cheese**
8 strips	**bacon,** cooked and halved
8 slices	**cooked turkey**
8	**sandwich-style pickle slices,** cut in half widthwise

In a large frying pan, melt 1 tablespoon butter and cook the onion, stirring frequently, until tender, about 5 minutes. Use a slotted spoon to remove onions to a separate dish and reserve. Do not wipe out pan.

Spread barbecue sauce on 4 slices of bread. Top each with 1 slice of cheese, 4 half strips of bacon, 2 turkey slices, and 2 pickle slices. Divide the onions among the sandwiches and top each with remaining cheese slices. Cover with remaining slices of bread.

Heat the frying pan over medium-low heat and melt the remaining 3 tablespoons butter. Cook sandwiches on both sides until golden brown and cheese is melted, about 3 minutes per side. Makes 4 servings.

BACON BUFFALO CHICKEN WRAPS

2 cups	**chopped cooked chicken**
$^1/_2$ cup	**buffalo wing sauce**
8 strips	**bacon,** cooked and crumbled
$^1/_2$ cup	**blue cheese dressing**
4 large	**flour tortillas,** warmed
4	**large Romaine lettuce leaves**
$^1/_2$ cup	**chopped celery**

In a medium saucepan, combine the chicken, wing sauce, and bacon, and cook over medium heat, stirring occasionally, until heated through, about 6 minutes. Remove from heat and cool for 5 minutes.

Drizzle the dressing evenly over each tortilla and top with a lettuce leaf. Spoon about $^1/_2$ cup chicken mixture down the center, and top with celery. Roll up tightly and cut each wrap in half on the diagonal. Makes 4 servings.

GRILLED B.A.M. SANDWICHES (BACON, AVOCADO, AND MUENSTER)

5 tablespoons	**butter,** softened, divided
1	**red onion,** sliced and separated into rings
8 slices	**sourdough bread**
8 strips	**thick-sliced bacon,** cooked and halved
8 slices	**Muenster cheese**
1	**avocado,** peeled, halved, and cut in $1/4$-inch slices

In a large frying pan, melt 1 tablespoon butter over medium heat and cook the onion, stirring frequently, until tender, about 5 minutes. Use a slotted spoon to remove onions to a separate dish and reserve. Do not wipe out pan.

Spread half the remaining butter on 4 bread slices. Flip bread over and top each with 4 halves of bacon, 1 slice of cheese, cooked onions, avocado slices, and another slice of cheese. Top with remaining 4 bread slices and spread remaining butter on the tops of each sandwich.

Heat a large frying pan over medium heat and cook the sandwiches, until both sides are golden brown and cheese has melted, about 3 minutes per side. Makes 4 servings.

THE ELVIS SPECIAL

5 tablespoons	**butter,** divided
2	**bananas,** peeled and cut in $1/4$-inch diagonal slices
$1/2$ cup	**creamy peanut butter**
8 slices	**white bread**
8 strips	**bacon,** cooked and halved

In a large frying pan over medium heat, melt 1 tablespoon of butter and cook the bananas, turning once, until lightly browned, about 4–5 minutes.

Spread the peanut butter evenly on 1 side of 4 bread slices. Top with fried banana slices, followed by 4 halves of bacon. Top with the remaining 4 bread slices. Spread the remaining 4 tablespoons butter on the tops and bottoms of each sandwich.

Heat a large frying pan over medium heat and cook the sandwiches, turning once, until golden brown, about 2–3 minutes per side. Makes 4 servings.

SLOW COOKER BACON
BARBECUE CHICKEN ROLLS

4	**boneless, skinless chicken breasts** (about 1 1/2 pounds)
2 cups	**barbecue sauce**
8	**large onion rolls,** split
3 tablespoons	**butter,** melted
16 strips	**bacon,** cooked and halved
2 cups	**grated cheddar cheese**

Place chicken breasts in a 3- to 4-quart slow cooker and pour barbecue sauce over top. Cook on low setting until chicken is tender and cooked through, about 6–7 hours. Remove chicken to a cutting board and cool for 15 minutes. Shred chicken with 2 forks and return to slow cooker.

Preheat oven to 425 degrees. Cover a baking sheet with aluminum foil. Arrange roll tops and bottoms cut-side up on pan and brush with the melted butter. Bake until edges are lightly browned, about 5 minutes. Transfer roll tops to a cooling rack. Using a slotted spoon, top each roll bottom with a generous spoonful of the chicken mixture. Layer each with 4 halves of bacon, and sprinkle with cheese. Return to oven and bake until cheese is melted, about 3–4 minutes. Replace roll tops and serve. Makes 8 servings.

BACON MUSHROOM MELTS

8 strips	**bacon,** halved
6 ounces	**thinly sliced mushrooms**
1/4 teaspoon	**pepper**
1/8 teaspoon	**salt**
2 tablespoons	**mayonnaise**
4 slices	**whole wheat bread,** toasted
4 slices	**tomato**
1/3 pound	**pepper jack cheese,** sliced

Preheat the oven broiler.

In a large frying pan over medium heat, cook the bacon until crisp. Transfer bacon to paper towels to drain, and discard all but 1 tablespoon of pan drippings. Return pan to heat and add the mushrooms, pepper, and salt, and cook, stirring occasionally, until lightly browned, about 5 minutes. Remove from heat and reserve.

Spread the mayonnaise over each slice of bread and arrange on a baking sheet. Spoon the mushrooms evenly over the bread and add a tomato slice. Arrange 4 halves of bacon over each tomato slice and cover with cheese slices. Broil until the cheese melts, 1–2 minutes. Makes 4 servings.

SIDE DISHES

BACON-WRAPPED CORN ON THE COB

8 strips **bacon**
8 **large ears sweet corn,**
husks and silk removed
freshly ground black pepper

Cut 8, 12-inch square pieces of heavy-duty aluminum foil. Spiral-wrap 1 strip of bacon around each ear of corn and place on a square of foil. Sprinkle with black pepper and wrap the corn securely in the foil, twisting the ends.

Preheat the grill to medium heat. Grill foil-wrapped corn, turning frequently, until corn is tender, about 15 minutes. Remove foil and return corn to grill, turning frequently, until bacon is crisp, 4–5 minutes. Makes 8 servings.

BACON AND PARMESAN HASSELBACK POTATOES

4	**large Yukon gold potatoes**
4 tablespoons	**cold butter**
	salt and pepper, to taste
8 strips	**bacon,** cut in 1-inch pieces
1/2 cup	**shredded fresh Parmesan cheese**

Preheat oven to 425 degrees. Line a baking sheet with aluminum foil.

Using a sharp knife, make 1/4-inch vertical cuts in each potato, without cutting all the way through the potato. Slice the butter into thin pieces and then cut in half. Place butter slices in alternating slits of each potato. Sprinkle with salt and pepper.

Place potatoes on prepared baking sheet and bake until skin is crispy and potato is tender, about 40–45 minutes.

Cook the bacon in a large frying pan over medium heat until golden brown. Transfer bacon to paper towels to drain. Reserve.

Remove potatoes from oven and cool on the pan for 10 minutes. Spread potatoes open and sprinkle with Parmesan cheese. Evenly divide the bacon into fourths and tuck the bacon pieces into the slits of each potato. Return the potatoes to the oven and bake until cheese melts, about 4 more minutes. Makes 4 servings.

CRUNCHY BACON AND ONION SNOW PEAS

6 strips	**bacon**
I pound	**snow peas,** stems and strings removed
	salt and pepper, to taste
I	**cup fried onions**

In a large frying pan over medium heat, cook the bacon until crisp. Transfer bacon to paper towels to drain; crumble and reserve.

Discard pan drippings and return pan to heat. Add the peas and cook over medium heat, stirring occasionally, until crisp-tender, about 2–3 minutes. Season with salt and pepper. Add reserved bacon and fried onions and cook, stirring, until heated through, about 2 minutes. Makes 6 servings.

BACON AND MUSHROOM STUFFING

1 1/4 pounds	**high-quality sandwich bread**
1 pound	**bacon,** chopped
2	**onions,** chopped
2 cups	**chopped celery**
1 pound	**sliced button mushrooms**
1 teaspoon	**dried thyme**
1 teaspoon	**dried sage**
1/2 teaspoon	**salt**
1/2 teaspoon	**pepper**
2 1/2 cups	**chicken stock or broth,** divided
2	**eggs**
1 1/2 teaspoons	**baking powder**

Preheat oven to 325 degrees. Remove crusts from bread, discard and cut remaining bread into 1/2-inch cubes. Spread on 2 baking sheets and bake until bread cubes are dry and crisp, stirring occasionally, about 25 minutes. Transfer to a large bowl.

In a large frying pan over medium heat, cook the bacon until crispy. Transfer bacon to paper towels to drain, and discard all but 2 tablespoons of pan drippings. Return pan to heat, and add onions and celery. Cook, stirring occasionally, until tender and lightly browned, about 8 minutes. Add mushrooms, thyme, sage, salt, and pepper, and cook until mushrooms are tender, about 10 minutes.

Preheat oven to 350 degrees. Lightly prepare a 9 x 13-inch baking dish with nonstick cooking spray. Add the mushroom mixture, and bacon to bread cubes; stir to blend. Stir in 2 cups chicken stock to combine. In a small bowl, whisk the eggs and baking powder until blended. Drizzle over stuffing mixture and stir. Add additional chicken stock if necessary so that all the bread is lightly moistened. Spread in prepared baking dish and bake until golden brown, about 1 hour. Makes 8–10 servings.

BRUSSELS SPROUTS WITH BACON

1 1/2 pounds **walnut-sized Brussels sprouts,** trimmed and halved
6 strips **bacon,** chopped
1 clove **garlic,** peeled and minced
freshly ground black pepper, to taste

In a steamer over boiling water, steam the sprouts for 5 minutes, or until just tender. While the sprouts are steaming, begin cooking the bacon in a large frying pan over medium heat, stirring often.

Drain the sprouts, shaking the strainer well. Carefully pour off the grease from the frying pan, making sure not to lose any of the bacon, and add the sprouts. Return to heat and cook, stirring occasionally, until bacon is crispy and sprouts are lightly browned. Add the garlic and cook, stirring constantly, for 1 minute. Sprinkle with black pepper and serve. Makes 6 servings.

BACON PULL-APART BREAD

1 pound	**frozen bread dough,** thawed
2 tablespoons	**unsalted butter,** melted, divided
1 envelope (1 ounce)	**ranch salad dressing mix**
8 strips	**bacon,** cooked and crumbled
1 cup	**grated Colby Jack cheese blend**

Lightly spray a large baking sheet with nonstick cooking spray.

On a lightly floured work surface, roll dough to a $1/2$-inch thickness and cut in 1-inch pieces. Roll each piece into a ball and place in a large bowl. Drizzle with 1 tablespoon melted butter and stir gently to coat. Measure out 1 teaspoon dressing mix and save for another purpose. Sprinkle the remaining mix over the dough balls and stir gently to coat. Add the bacon, cheese, and remaining melted butter; stir gently to coat. Arrange dough balls in a single layer, touching, in a 6 x 9-inch oval on prepared baking sheet. Cover and let rise in a warm area for 30 minutes, or until doubled in size.

Preheat oven to 350 degrees. Bake bread until golden brown, 20–25 minutes, covering with aluminum foil during the last 10 minutes to prevent over-browning. Remove from oven and use a large spatula to transfer the bread to a wire rack to cool. Makes 8–10 servings.

BACON AND ASPARAGUS SAUTE

1/3 cup	**white vinegar**
1 tablespoon	**sugar**
1/2 teaspoon	**dry mustard**
1/4 teaspoon	**pepper**
8 strips	**bacon,** diced
1 pound	**fresh asparagus,** trimmed and cut in 1 1/2-inch pieces
4 cups	**torn mixed salad greens**
1/2 cup	**sliced almonds**
2	**hard-cooked eggs,** peeled and sliced

In a small bowl, whisk together the vinegar, sugar, mustard, and pepper until combined; reserve.

In a large frying pan, cook bacon over medium heat until crisp. Transfer bacon to paper towels to drain, and discard all but 2 tablespoons of the pan drippings. Return pan to heat.

Saute the asparagus in the drippings over medium heat, stirring frequently, until crisp-tender, about 4–5 minutes. Add the vinegar mixture and cook, stirring, until slightly thickened and heated through, about 2 minutes. Remove from heat and cool for 5 minutes.

In a large salad bowl, combine the salad greens and almonds. Add the warm asparagus mixture and toss gently to combine. Arrange the sliced eggs on top and sprinkle with the bacon. Makes 6 servings.

BACON ROASTED BUTTERNUT SQUASH

8 strips	**bacon**
1	**butternut squash,** about 2$\frac{1}{2}$ pounds
$\frac{1}{4}$ cup	**maple syrup**
$\frac{1}{2}$ teaspoon	**salt**
$\frac{1}{2}$ teaspoon	**pepper**

Preheat oven to 350 degrees. Line a baking sheet with aluminum foil. Arrange the bacon on the baking sheet and cook until bacon is just starting to brown but not crispy, about 15 minutes. Remove from oven and transfer bacon to paper towels to drain. Pour the bacon drippings in a large bowl.

Increase oven temperature to 400 degrees. Lightly spray a 9 x 13-inch baking dish with nonstick cooking spray. Peel the squash and use a sharp knife to cut it in half lengthwise. Scoop out seeds and cut the squash into 1 $\frac{1}{2}$-inch cubes. Add the squash, maple syrup, salt, and pepper to the large bowl with the bacon drippings and stir to coat. Chop the bacon and stir into the mixture; spread in the prepared baking dish. Bake, stirring once during cooking, until squash is tender and bacon is crispy, about 30–40 minutes. Makes 6 servings.

BACON-STUFFED ARTICHOKES

6	**large artichokes**
3 cups	**seasoned breadcrumbs**
8 strips	**bacon,** cooked and crumbled
1/2 cup	**grated Parmesan cheese**
1/4 cup	**chopped flat-leaf parsley**
1 teaspoon	**chopped fresh thyme**
1/2 cup	**olive oil**
4 tablespoons	**butter,** melted
1/4 teaspoon	**freshly ground black pepper**

Cut stems from artichokes to leave a flat base. Use a sharp knife or kitchen scissors to cut off the pointed tip of each leaf. Spread the leaves apart and use a sharp spoon to scrape out the fuzzy choke. Set artichokes flat-side down in a large pot in a single layer. Add water to come 1 inch up the sides of the artichokes. Heat over medium-high heat until water comes to a simmer. Lower heat to medium-low, cover the pot and cook 15 minutes. Drain artichokes on paper towels and arrange flat-side down on a baking sheet.

Preheat oven to 350 degrees. In a large bowl, combine the breadcrumbs, bacon, Parmesan cheese, parsley, thyme, and olive oil; stir to blend. Gently spread apart the leaves of the artichokes and distribute the filling evenly between the leaves and in the artichoke centers. Drizzle with melted butter and sprinkle with pepper. Bake until artichokes are tender, topping is golden brown, and an outer leaf pulls off easily, about 20–30 minutes. Cool for 5 minutes before serving. Makes 6 servings.

GREEN BEANS WITH BACON, MAPLE, AND PECANS

3 tablespoons	**maple syrup**
2 tablespoons	**olive oil**
I tablespoon	**balsamic vinegar**
1/2 teaspoon	**Dijon mustard**
I clove	**garlic,** peeled and minced
I pound	**fresh green beans,** trimmed
8 strips	**bacon,** cooked and crumbled
	salt and pepper, to taste
1/4 cup	**chopped pecans,** toasted

In a small bowl, whisk together the maple syrup, olive oil, vinegar, mustard, and garlic; reserve.

Bring a large pot of water to boiling over medium-high heat, add the beans and cook until crisp-tender, about 4–5 minutes. Drain the beans in a colander and shake to dry.

Transfer the warm beans to a serving dish and drizzle with the maple syrup mixture. Add the bacon and stir to coat. Season with salt and pepper and garnish with pecans. Makes 6 servings.

SWEET POTATO, BACON, AND APPLE CASSEROLE

3 pounds	**sweet potatoes**
10 strips	**bacon,** chopped
2	**medium leeks,** washed well and thinly sliced
1	**large sweet apple,** such as Red Delicious, cored, peeled, and chopped
1 teaspoon	**brown sugar**
4 tablespoons	**butter**
1/2 teaspoon	**salt**
1/2 teaspoon	**pepper**
1 cup	**grated Colby Jack cheese,** divided

Preheat oven to 400 degrees. Scrub the potatoes, prick several times with a fork, and bake until tender, about 1 hour. Cool for 15 minutes.

Heat a large frying pan over medium heat and cook the bacon until crisp. Transfer bacon to paper towels to drain, and discard all but 1 tablespoon of pan drippings. Return pan to heat and cook the leeks and apples, stirring occasionally, for 4 minutes. Sprinkle with the brown sugar and continue cooking until apples are lightly browned and caramelized, 3–4 more minutes.

Prepare a 3-quart baking dish with nonstick cooking spray. Cut sweet potatoes in half and use a spoon to scoop cooked potato into a large bowl. Add butter, salt, and pepper, and mash with a potato masher until smooth. Add 3/4 cup of cheese, bacon, and apple mixture; stir to combine. Spread in prepared baking dish and sprinkle with the remaining cheese. Bake until hot and bubbling, about 20 minutes. Makes 8 servings.

DINNERS

GLAZED BACON DIJON PORK TENDERLOIN

6 strips	**bacon**
I	**pork tenderloin,** about I pound
1/4 teaspoon	**pepper**
1/4 cup	**packed dark brown sugar**
2 tablespoons	**apple juice**
I teaspoon	**Dijon mustard**

Preheat oven to 400 degrees. Line a baking pan with aluminum foil and spray with nonstick cooking spray.

Wrap bacon strips around tenderloin and secure with toothpicks. Transfer to prepared pan and sprinkle with pepper. Bake 20 minutes, or until an instant-read thermometer registers 135 degrees.

In a small saucepan over medium heat, combine the brown sugar, apple juice, and mustard; cook, stirring occasionally, until mixture comes to a boil. Remove from heat and reserve.

Remove tenderloin from oven and brush generously on all sides with the brown sugar mixture. Return to oven and cook 10 more minutes, or until an instant-read thermometer registers 145 degrees. Remove from oven and tent with aluminum foil. Let stand for 5 minutes before cutting into slices. Makes 4 servings.

BACON CHICKEN JALAPENO POPPER CASSEROLE

6 strips	**bacon,** diced
1	**onion,** chopped
2	**jalapenos,** seeded and finely diced
2 cloves	**garlic,** peeled and minced
8 ounces	**cream cheese,** softened
1/2 cup	**mayonnaise**
1 cup	**grated cheddar cheese**
2/3 cup	**grated Parmesan cheese,** divided
3 cups	**chopped cooked chicken**
1/2 cup	**crushed buttery crackers,** such as Ritz
4 tablespoons	**butter,** melted

Preheat oven to 375 degrees. Prepare a 9 x 13-inch baking dish with nonstick cooking spray.

In a large frying pan over medium heat, cook bacon until brown and crispy. Transfer bacon to paper towels to drain; crumble and reserve. Discard all but 1 tablespoon of pan drippings and return pan to heat. Add onion and jalapenos and cook over medium heat until onion is tender, 4–5 minutes. Add garlic and cook until fragrant, 1–2 minutes. Stir in cream cheese, mayonnaise, cheddar cheese, and 1/3 cup Parmesan cheese until cheese is melted and mixture is creamy. Add chicken and reserved bacon; stir to combine. Place chicken mixture in prepared pan.

In a medium bowl, combine cracker crumbs, remaining 1/3 cup Parmesan cheese, and melted butter and stir with a fork to mix. Sprinkle mixture evenly over top of casserole. Bake until bubbly and top is lightly browned, 25–35 minutes. Makes 8 servings.

BACON BBQ BRISKET

I can (8 ounces)	**tomato sauce**
$1/4$ cup	**ketchup**
$1/4$ cup	**packed dark brown sugar**
2 tablespoons	**balsamic vinegar**
I tablespoon	**lemon juice**
I tablespoon	**Worcestershire sauce**
2 teaspoons	**Dijon mustard**
I teaspoon	**hot sauce**
$1/2$ teaspoon	**liquid smoke flavoring**
$1/2$ teaspoon	**garlic powder,** plus extra for sprinkling
$1/4$ teaspoon	**salt,** plus extra for sprinkling
I	**flat-cut beef brisket** (4 pounds)
	freshly ground black pepper
I	**small Vidalia onion,** thinly sliced
6 strips	**bacon**

Preheat oven to 350 degrees. Line a shallow roasting pan with heavy-duty aluminum foil.

In a medium bowl, whisk together tomato sauce, ketchup, brown sugar, vinegar, lemon juice, Worcestershire sauce, mustard, hot sauce, liquid smoke, garlic powder, and salt until smooth.

Season both sides of the brisket with garlic powder, salt, and black pepper, to taste. Place brisket in prepared roasting pan fat-side down, and top with the onions. Drizzle the tomato sauce mixture over top of the brisket. Lay the bacon strips on top and cover pan tightly with aluminum foil. Roast until brisket is tender, $3 1/2$–4 hours, removing foil during last 15 minutes of cooking. Remove from oven, tent loosely with foil, and rest for 30 minutes before carving. Makes 8 servings.

ULTIMATE BACON-WRAPPED TURKEY

1	**turkey** (12–14 pounds)
16 strips	**bacon**
$^1/_2$ teaspoon	**freshly ground black pepper**
1	**onion,** coarsely chopped
2	**medium carrots,** peeled and sliced
2 stalks	**celery,** cut in 2-inch pieces
8 cloves	**garlic,** peeled
3 cups	**water**

Preheat oven to 350 degrees. Arrange the oven rack on bottom shelf of the oven. Fit a rack in a roasting pan. Rinse and dry the turkey and reserve the neck and giblets; tie the legs together.

Place a sheet of parchment paper on a baking sheet. Lay 8 bacon strips side by side to form a square. Using the other 8 strips of bacon, weave the bacon into a lattice pattern. Put the baking sheet in the freezer for 10 minutes, until bacon is firm. Remove from freezer and carefully lift bacon from the parchment. Arrange the bacon square like a diamond over the turkey, making sure the breast and legs are covered. Tuck excess bacon under the bird and sprinkle with pepper.

Place the turkey on the rack in the roasting pan and add the onion, carrots, celery, and garlic. Add water to the bottom of the pan. Cover the turkey loosely with aluminum foil and roast for 1 $^1/_2$ hours, rotating pan once during cooking, adding more water if necessary. Remove foil and continue cooking until an instant-read thermometer inserted in the thigh registers 165 degrees, about 1 $^1/_2$ hours. Rest the turkey for 20 minutes before carving. Makes 8 servings.

BACON, SPINACH, AND TOMATO CHEESE TORTELLINI

I package (20 ounces)	**refrigerated cheese tortellini**
2 tablespoons	**butter**
2 cloves	**garlic,** peeled and minced
3 tablespoons	**flour**
I teaspoon	**onion powder**
1 1/4 cups	**milk**
1/2 cup	**heavy cream**
I can (14.5 ounces)	**petite diced tomatoes,** with liquid
1 1/2 cups	**packed chopped fresh spinach**
3 tablespoons	**chopped fresh basil**
1/4 teaspoon	**salt**
1/4 teaspoon	**freshly ground black pepper**
8 strips	**bacon,** cooked and crumbled, divided
1/3 cup	**finely grated Parmesan cheese,** plus more for serving

Cook tortellini according to directions listed on package.

In a large saucepan over medium heat, melt the butter and add the garlic; cook, stirring, for I minute. Add the flour and onion powder and cook, stirring constantly for I minute. Slowly add the milk, whisking constantly. Add the cream and whisk until smooth. Cook, stirring constantly, until mixture begins to simmer; add the tomatoes with the liquid, spinach, basil, salt, and pepper. Cook until sauce thickens and spinach wilts, 2–3 minutes. Add all but I tablespoon of the crumbled bacon and the Parmesan cheese, and stir until cheese just begins to melt. Remove from heat.

Drain the tortellini, return to the pot and pour the sauce over top, stirring to coat. Serve immediately garnished with remaining crumbled bacon and additional Parmesan cheese. Makes 4–6 servings.

PESTO BACON CHICKEN

¹/₄ cup	**grated Parmesan cheese**
¹/₄ teaspoon	**garlic powder**
6	**boneless, skinless chicken breast halves,** pounded flat
	freshly ground black pepper
6 tablespoons	**prepared pesto sauce**
6 strips	**bacon**
¹/₄ cup	**olive oil**

Preheat oven to 400 degrees. Arrange a rack in a broiler pan.

In a small bowl, combine the Parmesan cheese and garlic powder; reserve.

Sprinkle the chicken breasts on both sides with pepper and spread one side of each breast with 1 tablespoon of pesto sauce. Roll up widthwise like a jelly roll, and wrap each roll with a bacon strip, securing with toothpicks. Arrange the chicken breasts on the rack in the broiler pan and sprinkle with olive oil.

Bake until the bacon is crispy and an instant-read thermometer inserted in the middle of the chicken registers 160 degrees. Remove from oven and sprinkle with the Parmesan cheese mixture. Return to oven and bake until cheese starts to melt, about 5 minutes. Makes 6 servings.

BACON BEEF BURGUNDY

8 strips	**bacon,** chopped
3 pounds	**beef chuck steak,** cubed
1 can (10.75 ounces)	**cream of mushroom soup**
1 cup	**Burgundy wine**
1 package (1 ounce)	**onion soup mix**
	freshly ground black pepper, to taste
	mashed potatoes or cooked noodles

In a large frying pan over medium heat, cook the bacon until it just begins to brown. Transfer bacon to paper towels to drain. Add the chuck steak to the hot drippings and cook, stirring occasionally, until meat is lightly browned, 8–10 minutes. Remove from pan and drain on paper towels.

In a 4- to 5-quart slow cooker, combine the bacon, beef, mushroom soup, wine, onion soup mix, and pepper. Cover and cook on low until meat is tender, 5–8 hours. Serve over mashed potatoes or hot cooked noodles. Makes 6–8 servings.

CREAMY BACON CORN SHRIMP RISOTTO

4 cups	**chicken stock or broth**
6 strips	**bacon**
$^1/_3$ cup	**finely chopped onion**
2 cloves	**garlic,** peeled and minced
I cup	**Arborio rice**
$^1/_2$ cup	**dry white wine**
$^1/_2$ teaspoon	**salt**
$^1/_4$ teaspoon	**pepper**
I cup	**fresh or frozen sweet corn kernels,** thawed
$^1/_2$ pound	**small cooked peeled shrimp,** chopped
I	**green onion,** finely chopped

In a medium saucepan, heat the stock over medium heat until it simmers; reduce heat to low, cover and reserve.

In a large frying pan over medium heat, cook bacon until brown and crispy. Transfer bacon to paper towels and drain; crumble and reserve. Discard all but 2 tablespoons of pan drippings and return pan to heat. Add onion and cook until tender, about 5 minutes. Add the garlic and cook I minute. Add the rice and stir for I minute. Add the wine, salt, and pepper. Continue cooking and stirring until most of the wine is absorbed.

Add the hot chicken stock $^1/_2$ cup at a time, cooking and stirring constantly until liquid is absorbed. Continue adding hot stock and stirring until risotto is creamy and tender (you may not need all of the chicken stock), about 25 minutes. Add corn, shrimp, and reserved bacon and cook until heated through, about 4–5 minutes. Garnish with green onions and serve. Makes 4 servings.

BACON CHEESEBURGER SOFT TACOS

1/4 cup	**mayonnaise**
2 tablespoons	**ketchup**
I tablespoon	**dill pickle relish**
I tablespoon	**vegetable oil**
2	**medium onions,** finely chopped
I pound	**lean ground beef**
I teaspoon	**prepared mustard**
1/4 teaspoon	**salt**
1/4 teaspoon	**pepper**
8	**small flour tortillas**
I cup	**grated cheddar cheese**
6 strips	**bacon,** cooked and crumbled
I cup	**finely chopped romaine lettuce**
I	**large tomato,** chopped

In a small bowl, whisk together the mayonnaise, ketchup, and relish. Cover and reserve.

Heat the oil in a large frying pan over medium heat and cook the onions, stirring occasionally, until tender, about 5 minutes. Add the ground beef, mustard, salt, and pepper, and cook, stirring occasionally, until beef is cooked through and no longer pink. Carefully drain grease from pan.

Spread the ketchup mixture on one half of each tortilla. Sprinkle cheese over the ketchup and top with the hot beef mixture. Top with bacon, lettuce, tomato, and more of the ketchup mixture if desired. Fold tortillas in half over filling and serve. Makes 8 servings.

BACON PEPPER JACK MAC AND CHEESE

2 cups	**uncooked elbow macaroni**
4 tablespoons	**butter**
1/4 cup	**flour**
1/2 teaspoon	**Worcestershire sauce**
1/2 teaspoon	**dry mustard**
1/2 teaspoon	**salt**
1/2 teaspoon	**pepper**
1 1/2 cups	**milk**
1/2 cup	**heavy cream**
3 cups	**grated pepper jack cheese**
8 ounces	**cream cheese,** softened
1 cup	**grated sharp cheddar cheese**
3/4 cup	**grated Parmesan cheese,** divided
8 strips	**bacon,** cooked and crumbled, divided
3/4 cup	**panko crumbs**
1 cup	**crushed cheddar french-fried onions**

Preheat oven to 350 degrees. Prepare a 2-quart baking dish with nonstick cooking spray. Cook macaroni according to package directions; drain and set aside.

In a large saucepan over medium heat, melt the butter. Add the flour, Worcestershire sauce, mustard, salt, and pepper, and whisk until smooth. Slowly add the milk and cream, whisking constantly. Bring to a boil; cook and stir for 1 minute, or until thickened. Stirring constantly, add the pepper jack cheese, cream cheese, cheddar cheese, and 1/2 cup Parmesan cheese; cook until melted. Add macaroni and all but 2 tablespoons of bacon; stir to combine. Transfer to prepared baking dish. Top with panko crumbs, remaining bacon, remaining Parmesan cheese, and onions. Bake, uncovered, until bubbly and golden brown, about 20–25 minutes. Makes 6 servings.

BACON-WRAPPED CHICKEN PINWHEELS

8 strips	**bacon**
4	**boneless, skinless chicken breast halves**
1/4 teaspoon	**salt**
1/4 teaspoon	**pepper**
1/2 cup	**cream cheese,** softened
1 can (4 ounces)	**chopped green chilies,** with liquid
2 tablespoons	**grated Parmesan cheese**
2 cloves	**garlic,** peeled and minced

Preheat oven to 375 degrees. Prepare a 9 x 13-inch baking dish with nonstick cooking spray.

In a large frying pan, cook bacon over medium heat until partially cooked but not crisp; drain on paper towels. Flatten chicken to 1/4-inch thickness. Sprinkle with salt and pepper.

In a small bowl, combine the cream cheese, chilies, Parmesan cheese, and garlic. Spread 1/4 of mixture on 1 side of each chicken breast. Roll up and tuck ends in. Wrap each chicken breast with 2 bacon strips and secure with toothpicks.

Arrange chicken in prepared baking dish and bake, uncovered, until juices run clear, about 35 minutes. Remove toothpicks and serve. Makes 4 servings.

BACON, BEEF, AND BEAN CASSEROLE

1/2 pound	**bacon,** diced
1/2 pound	**lean ground beef**
1	**large onion,** chopped
1 can (28 ounces)	**pork and beans**
1 can (15 ounces)	**kidney beans,** drained and rinsed
1 can (15 ounces)	**butter beans,** drained and rinsed
1/2 cup	**barbecue sauce**
1/2 cup	**ketchup**
1/2 cup	**sugar**
1/2 cup	**packed brown sugar**
2 tablespoons	**prepared mustard**
•2 tablespoons	**molasses**
1/2 teaspoon	**cumin**
1/2 teaspoon	**chili powder**
1/2 teaspoon	**salt**
1/2 teaspoon	**pepper**

Preheat oven to 350 degrees. Prepare a 3-quart baking dish with nonstick cooking spray.

In a Dutch oven or large frying pan, cook the bacon, ground beef, and onion over medium heat until bacon is lightly browned and beef is no longer pink. Drain grease from pan and add pork and beans, kidney beans, and butter beans.

In a medium bowl, whisk together the barbecue sauce, ketchup, sugar, brown sugar, mustard, molasses, cumin, chili powder, salt, and pepper. Add to beef mixture and stir well to combine. Transfer to prepared baking dish and bake, covered, for 45 minutes. Uncover and cook until mixture is hot and bubbling, about 15 more minutes. Makes 10 servings.

BACON, CHICKEN, AND NOODLES

I pound	**bacon,** chopped
3	**boneless, skinless chicken breast halves,** cut in 1-inch cubes
I	**large sweet yellow onion,** chopped
8 ounces	**sliced mushrooms**
I can (10.75 ounces)	**cream of mushroom soup**
I cup	**sour cream**
1/2 cup	**milk**
I teaspoon	**Worcestershire sauce**
1/4 teaspoon	**salt**
1/4 teaspoon	**pepper**
4 cups	**cooked egg noodles**

In a large frying pan, cook bacon over medium-high heat until crisp. Transfer bacon to paper towels to drain. Add chicken to hot drippings in pan and cook, stirring frequently, until cooked through and lightly browned, about 10 minutes. Carefully pour the grease from the frying pan and add the onion and mushrooms to the chicken and cook until onions are tender, about 5 minutes. Add soup, sour cream, milk, Worcestershire sauce, salt, pepper, and reserved bacon, and stir to combine. Cook, stirring frequently, until mixture is hot. Serve over hot cooked noodles. Makes 6 servings.

BACON GARLIC BUTTER SCALLOPS

1 pound	**scallops**
6 strips	**bacon,** diced
1/2 cup	**butter**
3 cloves	**garlic,** peeled and minced
1/2 teaspoon	**dried oregano**
1/2 teaspoon	**dried basil**
1/2 teaspoon	**crushed red pepper flakes,** optional
	salt and pepper, to taste
2 tablespoons	**chopped flat-leaf parsley**
	hot cooked rice

Remove small side muscles from scallops, if necessary; rinse in cool water, pat dry with paper towels and reserve.

In a large frying pan, cook bacon over medium-high heat until crisp. Transfer bacon to paper towels to drain, and discard all but 1 tablespoon of pan drippings; return pan to heat. Add butter and cook over medium heat until melted. Add garlic, oregano, basil, red pepper flakes, salt, and pepper. Cook, stirring frequently, until garlic is fragrant, about 2 minutes.

Add scallops and cook, turning once, until scallops are opaque and cooked through, 2–3 minutes per side. Add reserved bacon and cook for 1 minute. Garnish with parsley and serve over rice. Makes 4 servings.

SMOTHERED BACON AND ONION CHICKEN

8 strips	**bacon**
4	**boneless, skinless chicken breast halves**
1/4 teaspoon	**salt**
1/4 teaspoon	**lemon pepper seasoning**
1	**large onion,** sliced
2 tablespoons	**packed brown sugar**
1/3 cup	**grated Parmesan cheese**

In a large frying pan, cook bacon over medium-high heat until crisp. Transfer bacon to paper towels to drain; crumble and reserve.

Sprinkle chicken with salt and lemon pepper, and cook in the pan drippings over medium heat, turning once, until browned on both sides and an instant-read thermometer registers 165 degrees, about 6–7 minutes per side. Remove chicken to a heated dish, cover with aluminum foil, and keep warm.

Discard all but 2 tablespoons of pan drippings. Return pan to heat and cook the onion over medium heat, stirring occasionally, until tender and lightly browned about 6–7 minutes. Sprinkle with the brown sugar and continue cooking, stirring occasionally, until golden brown. Top each chicken breast with 1/4 of the crumbled bacon and 1/4 of the caramelized onions. Sprinkle Parmesan cheese over top and serve. Makes 4 servings.

BLT BOW TIE PASTA

8 strips	**bacon,** chopped
1	**small red onion,** chopped
2 cloves	**garlic,** peeled and minced
1/4 teaspoon	**red pepper flakes**
1 pint	**grape tomatoes,** chopped
1/2 cup	**heavy cream**
1/4 teaspoon	**salt**
1/4 teaspoon	**pepper**
12 ounces	**bow tie (farfalle) pasta,** cooked and drained
2 cups	**chopped arugula**
3 tablespoons	**chopped fresh basil**
1/4 cup	**grated Parmesan cheese**

In a large frying pan, cook bacon over medium-high heat until crisp. Transfer bacon to paper towels to drain, and discard all but 2 tablespoons of pan drippings. Return pan to heat and cook onion, garlic, and red pepper flakes over medium heat, stirring frequently, until onions are tender, about 5 minutes. Add tomatoes and cook, stirring occasionally, until tomatoes break down and thicken, about 10 minutes. Add the cream, salt, and pepper, and cook, stirring constantly, for 2 minutes. Add the cooked pasta, arugula, bacon, and basil. Stir to coat and sprinkle in Parmesan cheese. Makes 4 servings.

SLOW COOKER HEAVENLY BACON CHICKEN

8 strips	**bacon**
8	**boneless, skinless chicken breast halves**
I can (10.75 ounces)	**cream of chicken soup**
I can (10.75 ounces)	**cream of mushroom soup**
I cup	**sour cream**
$^1/_4$ cup	**flour**
$^1/_4$ teaspoon	**salt**
$^1/_4$ teaspoon	**pepper**
I pound	**egg noodles,** cooked and drained

In a large frying pan over medium heat, cook the bacon until it just begins to brown but is still flexible. Transfer bacon to paper towels to drain.

Wrap I bacon strip around each chicken breast and secure with toothpicks. Transfer to a 4- to 5- quart slow cooker.

In a medium bowl, whisk together the soups, sour cream, flour, salt, and pepper until well blended. Pour sauce over the chicken. Cover and cook on low until chicken and bacon are cooked and an instant-read thermometer insert into the chicken registers 160 degrees, about 5–8 hours. Divide the hot noodles among 8 heated plates and top with chicken. Whisk sauce and pour over chicken. Makes 8 servings.

DESSERTS AND SWEETS

BACON PEANUT BUTTER COOKIES

I pound	**bacon**
2 1/2 cups	**flour**
1/2 teaspoon	**baking powder**
1/2 teaspoon	**baking soda**
1/2 teaspoon	**salt**
1/2 cup	**butter,** softened
I cup	**packed dark brown sugar**
I cup	**sugar**
I cup	**smooth peanut butter** (not natural)
2 teaspoons	**vanilla**
2	**eggs**
I 1/2 cups	**salted shelled peanuts,** finely ground
	sparkling or raw sugar crystals, for sprinkling

In a large frying pan over medium heat, cook the bacon until crispy. Transfer to paper towels to drain; crumble into fine pieces. Allow the grease to cool in the pan for 5 minutes and pour through a strainer into a small bowl. Chill in the refrigerator for 30 minutes.

Heat oven to 350 degrees. Prepare a baking sheet with nonstick cooking spray. In a large bowl, combine the flour, baking powder, baking soda, and salt. In a medium bowl, beat the butter until creamy. Measure out 8 tablespoons of cooled bacon fat and add to the butter. Add the sugars, peanut butter, and vanilla; beat until creamy, about 3–4 minutes. Add the eggs, one at a time, beating after each addition. Beat in the flour mixture to blend and add the ground peanuts and bacon until combined. Shape dough into I 1/4-inch balls and place 2 inches apart on baking sheet. Dip a fork in warm water and flatten dough in a crisscross pattern. Sprinkle with sugar crystals. Bake until edges are just starting to brown, rotating halfway through baking, about 10–12 minutes. Cool on sheet for 2 minutes before transferring to a wire rack. Makes about 40 cookies.

MAN CANDY

1/3 cup	**dark beer**
1/4 cup	**packed dark brown sugar**
1/4 cup	**maple syrup**
1 pound	**thick-sliced bacon**
2 teaspoons	**pepper**

Preheat oven to 400 degrees. Line a rimmed baking sheet with aluminum foil.

Combine beer, brown sugar, and maple syrup in a small bowl, whisking well to dissolve sugar. Reserve.

Arrange the bacon on baking sheet, overlapping if necessary. Place in oven and cook for 10 minutes. Reduce temperature to 275 degrees, remove pan from oven, and blot the rendered fat from the bacon with a paper towel.

Brush one side of the bacon with the beer syrup. Flip, and coat the other side with the syrup. Return to oven and cook for 10 minutes. Remove from oven and brush both sides with syrup. Turn bacon over and cook for 10 minutes. Remove from oven, brush both sides with syrup and sprinkle with pepper. Turn bacon over and cook until crispy and browned, about 8 more minutes. Cool for 10 minutes before serving. Makes 6 servings.

BACON WALNUT MAPLE FUDGE

I cup	**packed dark brown sugar**
I jar (7 ounces)	**marshmallow creme**
I can (5 ounces)	**evaporated milk**
6 tablespoons	**butter**
1/8 teaspoon	**salt**
I bag (12 ounces)	**white chocolate chips**
I cup	**chopped walnuts**
I pound	**lean bacon,** cooked and finely crumbled
I teaspoon	**maple extract**

Line an 8 x 8-inch baking dish with aluminum foil, leaving a 1-inch overhang on all sides; spray with nonstick cooking spray.

Combine brown sugar, marshmallow creme, milk, butter, and salt in a heavy saucepan. Cook over medium heat, whisking often, until mixture comes to a boil. Boil for 5 minutes, stirring constantly to prevent scorching

Remove from heat and add the chocolate chips, stirring until fully melted and smooth. Stir in walnuts, bacon, and maple extract. Quickly pour into prepared pan and smooth the top. Refrigerate uncovered until firm, about 2 hours.

Use foil handles to lift fudge from pan. Remove foil and cut fudge in 1-inch squares. Serve at once or store in an airtight container in the refrigerator. Makes 64 pieces.

BACON BREAD PUDDING WITH VANILLA SAUCE

1 package (12-count)	**Hawaiian dinner rolls**
2 1/2 cups	**whole milk,** divided
1 cup	**heavy cream**
5	**eggs,** divided
1/2 cup	**sugar**
2 teaspoons	**vanilla,** divided
1/2 teaspoon	**salt**
1/4 teaspoon	**nutmeg**
8 strips	**bacon,** cooked and crumbled
1/2 cup	**packed dark brown sugar**
1 tablespoon	**flour**
1/4 teaspoon	**cinnamon**
2 tablespoons	**butter,** melted

One day before preparing recipe, cut the rolls in 1-inch cubes and arrange on a baking sheet. Dry for 24 hours.

Preheat oven to 350 degrees. Prepare an 8 x 8-inch baking dish with nonstick cooking spray. In a large bowl, combine 1 1/4 cups of milk, cream, 4 eggs, sugar, 1 teaspoon vanilla, salt, and nutmeg; whisk to blend. Add bacon and stir to combine. Arrange bread cubes in prepared dish and drizzle the egg mixture over top, stirring to coat bread evenly. Bake for 45 minutes, or until top is lightly browned and egg mixture is set.

In a large saucepan over medium heat, combine 1 1/4 cups milk, brown sugar, flour, cinnamon, 1 egg, and butter and whisk until smooth. Cook, whisking constantly, until mixture thickens and coats the back of a spoon, about 10–12 minutes. Stir in 1 teaspoon vanilla and remove from heat. Drizzle sauce over warm bread pudding to serve. Makes 8 servings.

MAPLE BACON CRUNCH

I can (8 ounces)	**refrigerated crescent seamless dough sheet or crescent rolls**
I pound	**bacon**
1/2 cup	**maple syrup,** divided
3/4 cup	**packed dark brown sugar,** divided

Preheat oven to 325 degrees. Line a rimmed baking sheet with parchment paper and spray with nonstick cooking spray.

Place the dough in prepared pan and press and stretch to a thickness of 1/4 inch. If using crescent roll dough, pinch perforations together. Prick all over with a fork.

In a large frying pan over medium heat, cook the bacon until it is just beginning to brown but not crispy. Transfer bacon to paper towels to drain. Cut the bacon in I-inch pieces and reserve.

Drizzle 1/4 cup of maple syrup evenly over the dough and sprinkle with 1/4 cup brown sugar. Arrange the bacon pieces on top, drizzle with remaining 1/4 cup maple syrup, and sprinkle with remaining 1/2 cup brown sugar.

Bake for 25 minutes, or until browned and bubbling. Remove from oven and cool in the pan to room temperature. Cut or break into pieces to serve. Makes 6 servings.

BACON MINCEMEAT TARTS

³/₄ cup	**flour**
¹/₂ cup	**sugar**
6 tablespoons	**butter,** softened
12 (3-inch)	**frozen tart shells**
1 ¹/₄ cups	**prepared mincemeat pie filling**
6 strips	**bacon,** cooked and finely crumbled

Preheat oven to 400 degrees.

In a small bowl, combine the flour, sugar, and butter, and blend with a pastry cutter or 2 forks just until the mixture looks like small peas; reserve.

Arrange the tart shells on a baking sheet and spoon 1 heaping tablespoon of mincemeat into each. Divide the bacon evenly among the tart shells and sprinkle on top of the mincemeat, pressing down gently. Sprinkle the top of each tart with a rounded tablespoon of the flour mixture. Bake for 15 minutes, or until edges of the pastry shell are lightly browned. Makes 12 servings.

NOTES

METRIC CONVERSION CHART

Volume Measurements			Weight Measurements			Temperature Conversion	
U.S.	**Metric**		**U.S.**	**Metric**		**Fahrenheit**	**Celsius**
1 teaspoon	5 ml		1/2 ounce	15 g		250	120
1 tablespoon	15 ml		1 ounce	30 g		300	150
1/4 cup	60 ml		3 ounces	90 g		325	160
1/3 cup	75 ml		4 ounces	115 g		350	180
1/2 cup	125 ml		8 ounces	225 g		375	190
2/3 cup	150 ml		12 ounces	350 g		400	200
3/4 cup	175 ml		1 pound	450 g		425	220
1 cup	250 ml		2 1/4 pounds	1 kg		450	230

Yum! Check out these "101" favorites
for more tasty recipes:

Each 128 pages, $9.99

Available at bookstores or directly from GIBBS SMITH
1.800.835.4993
www.gibbs-smith.com

ABOUT THE AUTHOR

Eliza Cross is an award-winning journalist and author of a dozen books, including *101 Things To Do With Bacon* and *101 Things To Do With a Pickle.* She is the founder of the bacon enthusiast society BENSA, and lives with her family in Denver, Colorado.